P9-CQS-557

DATE DUE		
JAN 8 '86	FEB 0 9 1987	DEC 0 1 1992
FEB 21 '86	JUN 1 2 1990	MAR 1 2 1993
SEP 25 1980		APR 0 8 1988
FEB 0 9 1987	APR 22 1994	
OCT 2 2 1987	OCT 1 2 1994	JUL 0 2 1998
DEC 1 8 1987		MAR 1 0 1999
OCT 2 5 1988	JUL 0 2 1997	OCT 0 8 1999
JAN 2 6 1989		
FEB 0 9 1989	SEP 2 9 1997	NOV 2 9 1999
OCT 1 8 1989	OCT 0 7 1997	
FEB 1 9 1990	NOV 0 5 1997	DEC 0 5 2000

NOV 1 6 2001

*Reginald Scot and
Renaissance Writings
on Witchcraft*

Twayne's English Authors Series

Arthur F. Kinney, Editor

University of Massachusetts, Amherst

TEAS 385

The diſcouerie

of witchcraft,

Wherein the lewde dealing of witches
and witchmongers is notablie detected, the
knauerie of coniurors, the impietie of inchan-
tors, the follie of ſoothſaiers, the impudent falſ-
hood of couſenors, the infidelitie of atheiſts,
the peſtilent practiſes of Pythoniſts, the
curioſitie of figurecaſters, the vanitie of dreamers, the begger-
lie art of Alcu-
myſtrie,

The abhomination of idolatrie, the horrible art of poiſoning, the vertue and power of
naturall magike, and all the conueiances
of Legierdemaine and iuggling are deciphered:
and many other things opened, which
haue long lien hidden, howbeit
verie neceſſarie to
be knowne.

Heerevnto is added a treatiſe vpon the
nature and ſubſtance of ſpirits and diuels,
&c : all latelie written
by Reginald Scot
Eſquire.

1. Iohn. 4, 1.

Beleeue not euerie ſpirit, but trie the ſpirits, whether they are
of God; for manie falſe prophets are gone
out into the world, &c.
1584

Reginald Scot and Renaissance Writings on Witchcraft

By Robert H. West

University of Georgia

Twayne Publishers • Boston

Reginald Scot and
Renaissance Writings on Witchcraft

Robert H. West

Copyright © 1984 by G. K. Hall & Company
All Rights Reserved
Published by Twayne Publishers
A Division of G. K. Hall & Company
70 Lincoln Street
Boston, Massachusetts 02111

Permission to quote from *Religion and the Decline of Magic* by Keith Thomas
(© 1971 Keith Thomas), was granted by Charles Scribner's Sons.

Book Production by Elizabeth Todesco

Book Design by Barbara Anderson

Printed on permanent/durable acid-free
paper and bound in the United States of
America.

**Library of Congress Cataloging in
Publication Data.**

West, Robert Hunter.
    Reginald Scot and Renaissance writings on witchcraft.

    (Twayne's English authors series; TEAS 385)
    Bibliography: p. 135
    Includes index.
    1. Witchcraft—History—16th century.
    2. Witchcraft—History—17th century.
    3. Scot, Reginald, 1538?–1599.
    I. Title.   II. Series.
    BF1571.W47   1984   133.4   84–9098
    ISBN 0–8057–6871–8

Contents

About the Author

Robert H. West is retired from the Department of English at the University of Georgia. He has three degrees in English from Vanderbilt University and is the author of three books on sixteenth- and seventeenth-century literature and demonology and of various articles. He served from private to captain in the United States Army Air Force throughout World War II.

Editor's Statement

Robert H. West's splendid reassessment of Reginald Scot demonstrates both how he was "as learned on occult matters as Robert Burton, as rational on them as Francis Bacon, and as consistent on the evidence as Pomponazzi," and how his enlightened views were almost a century ahead of most writers. But West's study is far more wide-ranging than this; by documenting the political, social, religious, and economic history of late Tudor and early Stuart England, West attempts a fresh and comprehensive analysis of witchcraft in the era of Elizabeth I and James I and the terror, arising from poverty and the Reformation, that made it such an explosive issue. In an era of fear and ferment, Scot remained level-headed and rational. "He unmasked the imposture and the delusion of the system [of witch trials] with a boldness that no previous writer had approached, and with an ability which few subsequent writers have equaled. Keenly, eloquently, and unflinchingly, he exposed the atrocious torments by which confessions were extorted, the laxity and injustice of the manner in which evidence was collected, the egregious absurdities that filled the writings of the Inquisitors, the juggling tricks that were ascribed to the Devil, and the childish folly of the magical charms. . . . If the question was to be determined by argument, if it depended simply or mainly upon the ability or the learning of the controversialists, the treatise of Scot would have had a powerful effect; it was by far the ablest attack on the prevailing superstition that had ever appeared." West's study makes frequent analogies with our own time, but its primary focus is on the Elizabethans: by showing how Scot was willfully misunderstood by King James and by William Perkins (and is still misinterpreted by historians of witchcraft today) West reveals a new writer whose thought and work demand a respect denied by centuries of abuse and neglect. This is a provocative and seminal study.

Arthur F. Kinney

Preface

The name Reginald Scot is not prominent in the annals of England. Even students concentrating in the sixteenth century are unlikely to hear more than a mention of it. Most historians have just glanced at Scot's work, for they hold it obsolete because its subject seems so. We all, indeed, have reason to think witchcraft an affliction of which society was long ago cured.

The witchcraft bacillus, nevertheless, is still alive and the antibody, witch-hunting, with its side effects, is always ready. Witchcraft is a kind of morally negative worldview, and with that infection anyone may be stricken in some form. Witch-hunting is a radical reaction to negativism and to the threats that it may foment and the contempt that it pours on more gracious opinions.

Neither witchcraft nor witch-hunting has been very successful in achieving its ends. But then, that can be said of most worldviews and the reactions to them. Christianity is the grandest case in point, and Hitler's reaction to it as a Jewish conspiracy managed early by St. Paul with intent to weaken gentile nations is analogous to western Europe's frenzy against witches. Such negativisms as witchcraft, together with the ensuing persecutions, are with us still, though the helpless witches for whom Scot sought some tolerance are no more and the particular oppression that he described has dwindled away.

Scot wrote with force and cogency about a basic human eccentricity whose manifestations, real or imagined, aroused fear and revulsion. Serious witchcraft expresses a primitive sense of the mystery of existence and a restless effort to adapt profitably to menace in it. Witch-hunting expresses a kindred sense of mystery and a shrinking from it as it appears in the witch's frightening adaptation.

Scot's major effort was to defuse the witch craze by denying the existence of "serious" witchcraft. As his sixteenth- and seventeenth-century critics repeatedly said, he tried to confound witchcraft with cozenage. He meant to take the dread out of it and the dignity, and to leave it a sham not worth persecuting. This was an effort very much ahead of his time. The profit that the witch realized, he argued, was not wonder-working power or occult insight, but an ephemeral worldly advantage from trickery.

The mystery, though, whether or not menacing, may shine through Scot's pragmatic overlay. Our existence borders everywhere on the unknown, and Scot was in his own way fascinated with it, although he looked into it with an honesty and a common sense that dissipated most of the official answers of demonology.

Reginald Scot and Renaissance Writings on Witchcraft is an effort to show Scot in relation to his own time and to subsequent ones. It treats his response to the much-voiced views of witch-hunters and to the obscure ones of witches. It examines the opinions of modern historians in relation to those of Scot, and the responses to him made by seventeenth-century witch writers. Scot wrote against many earlier writers, and many later ones against him. Those whom he resisted included Jean Bodin, one of the foremost intellectuals of his time, and those who resisted Scot included lordly scholars of great reputation and following. He had his supporters, too—less august than his foes and fewer. This book tries to touch, at least, upon the more prominent of both sorts.

The organization of Scot's *Discovery* is journalistic. Arguments and examples pile up in staccato succession, and repetition is plentiful. An idea may dodge through many chapters, surfacing and resurfacing as Scot's thought of the moment calls it up. Thus his central contention—that devils cannot act in the physical world and so were no help to witches—is scattered in short passages throughout the book. Sometimes, therefore, quotations may be juxtaposed here that in the original are widely spaced.

Scot did not depend wholly on his radical assertion about devils, but readied fall-back positions: (1) that much witchcraft was generally admitted to be fraudulent; (2) that the witch was so ignorant that she could not associate guiltily with devils even if solicited; (3) that to magnify witch marvels was to depreciate those of prophets, Apostles, and of Christ himself; (4) that belief in witch marvels was idolatrous; (5) that belief in the possibility of a really operative witch's pact showed a lack of confidence in Christian baptism; (6) that fear of devils and witches showed a failure of faith in God; and (7) that a witch on trial ought in justice to have all the consideration that law provided for those accused of other crimes.

Most of these arguments are out of date now, but they affirmed Scot's own Christian faith and showed how he fitted into it the hard structure of his skepticism on witches. Scot's stand is not, granted his polemical requirements, disagreeable to a modern Christian confronted with our curious twentieth-century revival of witchcraft and Satanism. Scot's opinions are not now so obsolete as his subject has led many to suppose.

Robert H. West

University of Georgia

Acknowledgments

The chief help that I must acknowledge for the book is from Mr. Arthur F. Kinney, a distinguished editor and scholar in Renaissance studies and field editor in the Renaissance for the Twayne Series. He suggested the subject and has made numerous and useful suggestions and alterations in the typescript. Professor Thomas J. Stritch of the University of Notre Dame read an early version and contributed helpful encouragement and comments. Ms. Emily McKeigue, associate editor of Twayne Press, has been prompt and kindly, as has Ms. Elizabeth B. Todesco, who did the arduous work of bringing my typescript into form. Mr. Thomas V. Lange, Assistant Curator of Rare Books at the Huntington Library, provided the frontispiece from the library's fine copy of Scot's *Discovery.* Staff members of the University of Georgia Library borrowed for me a hard-to-find book, and Ms. Karen Chittenden of The Folger Shakespeare Library provided an indispensable microfilm.

Chronology

ca. 1538 Reginald Scot born, probably on the estate of his father, Richard Scot, in Kent.

ca. 1555 Entered Hart Hall, Oxford, but left without a degree.

1568 Married Jane Cobbe on October 11, and settled at Smeeth, Kent.

ca. 1574 Daughter Elizabeth born.

1574 *A Perfect Platform of a Hoppe Garden* published in London.

1575 Succeeded to a small part of an aunt's estate.

1576 Second edition of *A Hoppe Garden.*

1578 Third edition.

ca. 1578 Appointed a Justice of the Peace.

1584 Published *The Discovery of Witchcraft.*

ca. 1584 Married a widow named Alyce, last name unknown.

1586–1587 Collector of Subsidies for the Lathe of Shepway.

1588 Member of Parliament for New Romney.

1588 Perhaps captain of untrained foot soldiers assembled against the Armada.

1599 Died on October 9, allegedly at Smeeth.

Chapter One

Witchcraft in Scot's Time

In the twenty-fourth year of Queen Elizabeth I's reign (1582) an Essex justice of the peace examining a suspected witch told her ominously that from the Continent there is "a man of great cunning and knowledge, come over lately unto our Queen's Majesty, which hath advertised her what a company of witches be within England: whereupon I and other of her Justices have received commission for the apprehending of as many as are within these limits."[1]

What cunning and knowledgeable man the justice had in mind is not certainly known, and indeed he may have been fictitious. But the idea that the Continent was a source of knowledge on witchcraft was perhaps widespread in England, dating from Elizabeth's succession and the return of influential Protestants who had fled Queen Mary's drastic reestablishment of Catholicism.[2] Among them was John Jewel, who presently became Elizabeth's bishop of Salisbury. In an early sermon before the queen, Jewel warned her majesty that "witches and sorcerors . . . within the last few years are marvellously increased within your grace's realm" and that from their doings "Your grace's subjects pine away even unto death. . . ."[3]

Jewel probably qualified in the eyes of most hearers as "a man of great cunning and knowledge" about witches,[4] for he had lived and traveled in Germany, then convulsed by witch alarms and prosecutions. He had presumably heard much evidence that witches cause people to pine away; and he must also have seen some of the accused themselves pine most miserably under the attentions of jurists convinced of witchcraft's evils. Although the persecutions in Germany were by no means at their peak in the 1550s, they were monstrously prominent. A single town is said to have needed eight executioners to keep up with the work.[5]

Whether or not Bishop Jewel's sermon was influential in the

reading before Parliament in 1559 of a law that made witchcraft
a felony, it certainly was one signal of the arrival in England
of something of the Continent's excitement about witches. The
uproar never attained in England anything like the Continental
volume, but it does seem to have waxed noticeably in the 1560s
and 1570s, as the English conception of witchcraft gradually
took on some lurid features common in Germany and France.

Basic Dogmas

Continental authorities on the ways of witches and their reasons were largely agreed throughout the sixteenth century and
most of the next that the witches' chief reason for witchcraft
was attachment to the most horrid of heresies, the Satanic, and
that the witches' ways were those of a hell-born conspiracy for
bringing all mankind to worship of Satan and so to damnation.
Every true witch supposedly signed a pact with a devil in person,
then periodically traveled to gatherings called Sabbats for abject
reaffirmation of loyalty and for perverted jollification. At home
the witch performed *maleficia,* the evil deeds against her neighbors by which she gratified both her own malice and that of
her demon master, once again confirming her service to him.
The devil might at request change her shape, carry her through
the air, bring on bad weather. And he might sicken men and
animals and sometimes slay them.

When Bishop Jewel began stirring up England not all of the
Continental charges were familiar to English law, to the masses
of the people, or, it would appear, to local witches themselves.
The masses were uninstructed in it, and the law so far as it
touched village witchcraft was concerned almost entirely with
the *maleficium.* The witches certainly did try sometimes to perform objectionable feats upon a neighbor's goods or person,
but they did not ordinarily confess to formal pacts with devils,
nor did they travel to Sabbats. They acted individually, for the
most part by traditional or idiosyncratic folk means to afflict
neighbors—or perhaps as often to relieve them, for many of
England's practicing witches were "white" ones and professed
only to expose bewitchment and break spells, find lost or stolen
belongings, and tell personal fortunes. Although the idea of
witches as servants of Satan was abroad in the land generally,

neither the rural witches nor their victims or customers or prosecutors necessarily thought of the craft's charms and sigils as direct from the devil's hand or as pulsing with his power. English statutes on witchcraft make no mention of pact until 1604, when Parliament under James I replaced Elizabeth's law with a more severe one aimed at all who "covenant with any evil or wicked spirit." Although indictments before 1600 usually contained the formula "seduced by instigation of the devil" and an occasional one mentioned "imps, otherwise spirites," as familiars or servitors of witches, they said nothing explicit about the Sabbat, and any implication of a Satanic conspiracy was just a form customary in most of the age's complaints about any sort of sin. England was resistant to Continental-style credulity and panic about Satan's most direct and most advertised assault upon humanity. But it was not immune.

Refinements of Dogma

In England as on the Continent, the literate classes did rationalize witches' doings largely according to St. Thomas Aquinas's wonderfully coherent thirteenth-century articulations of spirits and their human contacts. Since the source of the startling powers attributed to witches could not be divine, it had to be demonic.[6] Since men could not by either natural means or allowed sacerdotal ones coerce demons for private purposes, any men who had demonic service must have got it by somehow submitting their purposes to those of demons. In substance such submission meant worship, which, of course, brought in the idea of pact, for worship of Satan broke the baptismal covenant with God. To the idea of pact some fifteenth-century witchhunters attached that of the Sabbat and hell's special recruitment among God's baptized on behalf of a malefic organization.[7] Into the towering rationalization of these "Inquisitors" learned people could fit folk magic neatly enough, but it was by no means native there, especially in England. The system was not well known to witches in England nor to their ordinary clients and victims.

Ritual magic. The practice that theologians designed their system to describe was, in fact, not primarily witches' magic as seen in the countryside but the Dr. Faustus–style thaumaturgy

that openly invoked devils by sophisticated means for such large
purposes as the finding of great treasure. It served, too, those
who sought power through influence with rulers or perhaps
by their ritual murder. English laws that condemned contact
with spirits were aimed chiefly at this ambitious, politically ori-
ented sorcery. Dr. John Dee, when Astrologer Royal to Queen
Mary, was once charged with enchantments against her life.[8]
Elizabeth's ministers feared such a threat to her, especially from
sympathizers with Mary Queen of Scots, and on that account,
perhaps, pushed the 1563 law that made a felony "any Invoca-
tions or Conjurations of evil and wicked Sprites, to or for any
Intent or Purpose." In the lawmakers' anxiety about supernatural assault upon high-placed persons the primitive conjurations
of country witches might well go unrebuked.

   Magician and witch.   The distinction of witch from magician was not, nevertheless, a fixed one in demonology, either
English or Continental, for both the witch and the magician
tried, after all, to tap supernatural currents of power, though
the witch worked on a low level. Both could do mysterious
bad turns or what might seem good ones. Both used signs and
incantations (or at least mutterings) that were strange to the
uninitiated. And every operation of both was at bottom quickly
suspect as worshipful cooperation with devils. The gap, then,
between the folk spells of the ignorant witch and the elaborate
rituals of the learned mage could not at last exempt either witch
or magician from a charge of demonolatry. To most persons
competent to scrutinize it, the case against the witch and that
against the magician seemed finally one, and all but unargua-
ble—as indeed it was, granted the time's theological grounds.

   Witches and those erroneously accused of being witches did
not, usually, know enough about the theology that indicted them
to dispute it strongly. Magicians did know enough, and their
basic defense was a counterclaim, dimly Neoplatonic in form.
Theologians erred, magicians said, in thinking that well-initiated
enchanters could not constrain devils. By ancient and allowable
rites mighty with divine names and with prayers to good angels
who controlled devils, magicians blamelessly prevailed over hell
much as priestly exorcists did. This claim and related ones, together with ties to influential clients, seem usually to have pro-
tected known magicians from the law.[9] But the indicted witch
of village or slum, neither clearly grasping the substance of

her indictment nor powerfully backed, became more defenseless as the charge of demon worship grew in England to underlie increasingly the traditional one of *maleficium,* that is, of injury by occult means. Although sixteenth-century English prosecutors rarely pushed the charge of Satanic heresy with anything like the intensity customary on the Continent,[10] still even unmentioned before judge and jury the charge added to the public horror of witchcraft and encouraged the courts to deal harshly. The witch craze never approached in England the frenzy common for decades in parts of France and Germany. But the literate Englishman did share with his counterpart abroad an acquaintance with the orthodox theory of magic and witchcraft as demonic heresy, and many localities suffered something of the Continental outrage at those who "sold" themselves to the devil.

The Background in Demonology

In England, then, as elsewhere, a willful human approach to Satan's destructive angels was the heart of sixteenth-century theory on witchcraft and an element in law on it and in popular concern about it. Assertion of contact with nonhuman spirits of various kinds has, of course, been common to all the tribes of men. Whether or not belief in contact rested on real experience, always many persons (some believers, some doubters, some simply frauds) have professed to know about spirits and have provided information aplenty on gods, daemons, fairies, elves, nymphs, sylphs, imps, naiads, elementals, undines, and a dozen other sorts of mostly invisible but constantly active creatures with special powers, both natural and supernatural. In the pagan Mediterranean world near the time of Christ, gods of many nations (the Olympians of Greek and Roman mythology most prominent to us) were supposedly interested in human affairs. Intermediate between gods and man was a class of spirits or demispirits that the Greeks called daemons. These beings could appear to men and could manage physical things in a superhuman way. Classifications of them were, not surprisingly, very loose and shifting, and they overlapped in various perplexing ways.

Two demonologists. The sixteenth-century authors on spirits most read in England usually at least brushed through antiquity's account of daemons to show how it linked to Chris-

tianity's and how wrong part of it was. Thus the most influential
of French demonologists, the celebrated jurist Jean Bodin, explains in chapter 1 of his *De la Demonomanie des Sorciers* that
holy scripture and nearly all sects of ancient philosophers—Platonists, Aristotelians, Stoics, Arabs—are agreed that spirits exist;
the atheistic Epicureans' doubt of it goes against all metaphysics
and the existence of God. Plato, Plutarch, Iamblichus, and Plotinus, Bodin said, held that some daemons were good and some
bad; but Christians use the word *demon* always for evil spirits.
Another demonologist of the time, Johann Weyer, disagreed
strongly with Bodin about witches but sketched ancient demonology much as Bodin did. "Philosphers," he said, thought some
daemons good and some bad, some mortal and others immortal.
Platonists claimed that the immortal were powerful, companion-
able to men, and partly good, partly evil. All philosophers
thought them prone to take part in magic. The famous Neoplatonist Iamblichus says that bad daemons lend themselves to evil
deeds. They are crafty and in their apparition fantastic. Men
can detect them by their characteristic claim to be gods or good
spirits and to demand worship, which, Weyer is quick to say,
no Christian should give.[11]

Demonolatry. In this negation Weyer was close to the
early church. From its beginning Christianity frowned on contacts with finite spirits except those sent from God. As a mono-
theism Christianity could not countenance the sort of adoration
that Neoplatonist magicians were willing, in polytheistic style,
to pay to the spirits they tried to evoke. The Neoplatonist philosophers professed an elevated sort of magic through good daemons that aimed at what amounted to a minor self-deification.
Proclus, who like Iamblichus was much studied by Renaissance
humanists, told how ancient Egyptian priests used natural objects
and sacrificial "animals appropriate to the gods" to acquire "the
powers of daemons" and so learned about higher daemons "to
whom they drew near." From such spirits they proceeded to
"the very powers and actions of the gods. Partly by learning,
with the daemons their teachers, and partly . . . by interpreting
the appropriate symbols . . . they ascended to the peculiar intel-
ligence of the gods; and at last, when . . . in large part the
daemons had been laid aside, they moved into the fellowship
of the gods."[12]

Such moral and theological refinement of magic as Proclus wrote of could not attract the many practitioners who were intent less on spiritual improvement than on worldly advantage. With some reason Christians suspected all magicians of inviting daemons primarily for returns in money, promotions, revenges, reputation, and sexual scoring. To St. Paul and to the Church Fathers, spirit magic was diabolism, alliance with the evil principle, devotion to God's enemy. And so it remained, with adjustments, into the Middle Ages, when Scholasticism, in agreement with St. Augustine, confirmed the wrongness of nearly all pagan usage on the subject; daemons and pagan gods alike it accused as actually being demons, devils, those spirits who rebelled with Satan.

Belief in Spirits

In Elizabeth's England a well-educated man certainly knew some classical writers on daemons (Plutarch, Apuleius); and he knew something of Augustine, Tertullian, Origen, and other Fathers of the Church who wrote on angels, fallen and unfallen, as well as Aquinas and Calvin. He might have read, too, some of Marsilio Ficino's fifteenth-century translations of Iamblichus and Proclus, and perhaps some of Johann Reuchlin and Pico della Mirandola on the Jewish Cabala, newly important to Christians, which had much to say of spirits and magic. In London this cultivated Elizabethan might know personally such variously practicing magicians as Dr. John Dee and Simon Forman. He was sure to have some acquaintance with the *Occult Philosophy* of the early sixteenth-century "magician" Henry Cornelius Agrippa, and with his "recantation" of magic in *The Vanity of the Arts and Sciences*. Almost anywhere in the country he could have heard sermons on spirits from such preachers as the Calvinist William Perkins.

This Elizabethan, then, was pretty sure to believe that such "spiritual creatures" as Dr. Dee thought he heard sometimes in his house at night and as Jean Bodin saw spherically shining in his room could appear anywhere, some to hurt men, some to help. He could speak on their approaches, their powers, and their purposes, and on the tricks of the evil ones. A dim notion of all this the literate man might help to trickle down to the common people so that they too could grasp something of hell's most literal threat to them and of the rather meager-seeming succor that heaven might extend.

For their part the common people provided the educated ones with homely instances: Robin Goodfellow and the faeries of the glades; devil dogs and devil cats; strange seizures; prodigies glimpsed in skies or waters. And curses not loud but deep, brought on by daily friction in village or slum life. Images thrust through with pins. Ailments beyond the physician's practice and seeming accidents at which crones chuckled maliciously.

English folk magic undertook such minor efforts as frustrating churners and killing stock. Mockingly it rendered men impotent and women barren. It sickened some persons and slew others— or so dozens of indictments averred. The least of these deeds could terrify those at hand for it; and after all, it was as attributable to Satan as the killing of kings and the swaying of battles. Clergymen and officials of the law could, then, often successfully associate witchcraft in villagers' minds with Satan's malice and power.

A woman confessed to a justice of the peace that a spirit "called Suckin, being black like a dog" had taken her "by the coat" and asked whether she "would go with it." Later she sent its companion, Lierd, to kill a neighbor's beasts, but instead it "plagued Byett's wife to death." A boy, son of accused parents, testified that a spirit "took him by the left leg and also by the little toe, which was like his sister, but that it was all black." When he cried out, his father said to his mother, " 'Why, thou whore, cannot you keep your imps from my children,' whereupon she presently called it away. . . ."13

Grotesque as such witnessing was, the elements of the scholastic account of fallen angels rode easy enough upon it. Suckin and Lierd and the black imp who took a toe-hold may have been lowly devils, but that they could do evil deeds, even killing, was easy to believe.

Development of demonology. Thomistic angelology had it that all angels, good or bad, were bodiless intellects, created originally in ranks and orders to praise God and be his messengers. From their first existence angels knew men and the world by a divinely implanted grasp of species. They could show themselves to human beings by intruding into minds and manipulating faculties. Or by the control of "local motion" they could fashion "vehicles," usually vaporous ones, in which to appear, speak, and act. After expulsion from heaven, Satan and his angels retained their ranks, their specific knowledge of created beings, and their power to move matter locally and to enter human minds. They could not control the human will or genuinely transform bodies, but they could stir the humors, the appetites, and the fancy to delude men in various ways. They had not constant or unchecked power to do physical harm, but by God's permission, overt or tacit, they could mightily trouble those whom providence had scheduled for test or punishment. Dwelling on these matters, a man might feel himself delivered to hell's encroaching malice.

Although the medieval foundation studies of demonology were, of course, Catholic, learned Protestants hastened to make their modifying contributions. Many of them varied from the great scholastics chiefly in insistence that scripture had to be the sole source of fact so that they professed to frown on extensive speculation about such matters as demonic substance and orders. The first translation of an influential Protestant demonological specialist work into English, *A Dialogue of Witches* (1575), by the French cleric Lambert Daneau, makes a great display of despising detailed exposition of the nature of devils. A certain Spanish Jesuit, says one of Daneau's speakers, has disputed "so curiously of this whole argument, that he weried his hearers, . . . proposing this openly, and publishing a Booke, wherein he professeth that he will intreate of Deuilles." The interlocutor agrees that their discussion should not go into "these vayne babling proofes" since out of them only vanity arises. He will not try to say what devils there be, or how many, how the sorts differ, their colors and humors, and other trifling matters, which "by them is most exquisitely and diligently handled, which would be accompted of the most subtile sort among the scholastical doctores." As for him, he abhors devils and knows them only from the word of God. If "the philosopher Iamblichus with his monstrous religion, if Proclus . . . have waded anything deeper into knowledge of these things, or with more diligence sought out the secretes of deuels . . . I enuie not at it, and I easily yield them the knowledge of such oglie matters."[14]

Daneau goes on at considerable length, nevertheless, about the relations of devils to witches. But probably his declared reticence on some established articles of demonology was, after all, an influence for skepticism, though in the mouth of a man basically as credulous as any.

Revival of Pagan Demonology

Scholastic demonology and the modified Protestant versions of it were not the only theories in the Renaissance of spirits at work. The humanist revivals of Neoplatonism and the Cabala began a partial absorption of both into Christian thought and a reinvigoration of the earlier pneumatology, which awarded angels (once again called daemons)[15] a much larger role in the routine management of the physical world than scholasticism did and which elaborated the means of human access to them. It played down the fall of angels and the mortal peril of traffic with the fallen; and it held good and evil daemons, creatures intermediate between God and men, to have rank and power according to function in the emanated universe. Even top-ranked daemons (pagan Neoplatonists had called them gods) were approachable through religious rite, and a magus strengthened by his communion with them could rise in the way that Proclus described from rank to rank toward knowledge of God—and incidentally he could do physical marvels through daemonic powers exerted at his instance. For apparition daemons did not have to assume temporary and unvitalized vehicles such as Aquinas postulated but had true personal bodies, compressible at will into solidity from their varying degrees of rarefaction.

Upon this intrusive daemonology such Renaissance Christian Hermeticists and Cabalists as Pico, Reuchlin, Giordano Bruno, and Agrippa largely rested their accounts of "theurgy," ceremonial "high" magic. They did not absolutely gainsay Christian orthodoxy if they could help it, but they shaded their demonology away from the Thomistic pattern to one that made their traffic with spirits seem more allowable than clerical authority, either Catholic or Protestant, approved. In their track came the nameless writers on low magic, the frankly power-and-riches-bent authors of handbooks spuriously attributed to Agrippa, Peter of Abano, King Solomon, various popes, and others. These "grimoires" of the "goetists" (black magicians) were full of reckless incantations for greedy purposes.

The Magical Conceit

In sixteenth-century England treasure hunting by means of magic was endemic.[16] A deposition of 1510 tells how two priests persuaded some laymen to seek a treasure that a person since dead had glimpsed. It was a chest full of gold with a devil sitting on it. Experimentally poked with a sword, the devil had "nipped it asunder . . . as it had been a rush." To be rid of this guardian the two priests provided various magical implements: "a circle of virgin parchment," a "great mass book," a "thing gilt of a foot long like a holy water strynkill, and frankinsense, with diverse books of their craft." They drew three circles of thirty feet in diameter for their lay partners to stay safe in and invoked spirits called Belphares and Obirion. Nothing worked. They could not locate the chest. But they did arouse the law, and an ecclesiastical court imposed penance on each of them.[17] Abysmally astray as this goetical venture sounds to us, it evidently operated far more elaborately than village witchcraft did.

Much of the joy of a man learned in magic and spirits seems to have come from his cultivated sense of superiority to the mass of humanity and even to other more conventionally schooled persons than he. Pico challenged the whole literate world with his celebrated 900 theses, and Bruno in the *Heroic Frenzies* asserted the emancipation of the Hermetic magician from the restraints that bound lesser persons. A phase of this pride of profession was a tendency to deny all standing in magic to the folk witch and all sound knowledge of it to divines, who ought, Paracelsus said, to study it—not for use but just for understanding.[18] Agrippa once defended a woman accused of witchcraft and got her off with the insistence that her accusers, who had apparently used a celebrated Scholastic handbook of witchcraft, were as contemptibly ignorant of magic as she was. To the believer in great daemons as managers of creation on behalf of a rather remote God, the notion that an unread witch could seriously influence the spirit world was foolish and derogatory.[19]

Limited Skepticism

Oddly enough, then, Hermetic and Cabalistic magicians, the most assiduous of dealers with spirits, encouraged a kind of skepticism about witchcraft. Agrippa's pupil, Johann Weyer, was the leading Continental rejecter of the description of witchcraft that orthodox prosecutors used. Weyer doubted neither the temporal activities of the devil and his angels nor men's effective and heinous cooperation with them. But an old woman accused as a witch was, Weyer insisted, too witless either to use spirits or be used by them except as a helpless pawn.[20] She could not make any pact with Satan that would bind either of them, nor could she move him to do anything for her or against others except the evil deeds he would want to do anyway. Whatever a devil shrewdly did in witches' names, then, was chargeable solely to him. The only human beings really guilty of devilry, Weyer insisted, were the "magiciens infames," who indeed by their wicked rites bound the devil to themselves and themselves to him. Weyer did not quite eliminate from his thinking the black magician's excuse that he had some real power to coerce spirits. But he did deny that the spirits concerned were ever good angels, and he insisted that the goetist's rites amounted to a tacit pact or at least were desperately guilty. Thus Weyer continued a version of Agrippa's devaluation of folk magic, with pity for those accused of it and disdain for orthodox Catholic theory of it. Unlike Agrippa, Weyer dwelled almost entirely on magic low and black. But, like Agrippa, he expressed belief in ritual magic and unbelief in witchcraft.[21]

Weyer was a fervent Lutheran and made a strong element in his defense of witches the Protestant rejection of "priest magic." Such rejection was an influential though anomalous element in the general growth of skepticism regarding spirits and magic. If the comfortable practices of praying and vowing to saints, angels, and the Virgin, of wearing amulets, and of making the sign of the cross and calling on Christ's name were held to be vain, illicit, or even fraudulent, the whole idea of the intervention of spirits in men's affairs at men's solicitation lost some credibility. By sneering at direct and seemingly simple religious protections against the powers of darkness and at the same time proclaiming the active and literal assaults of those powers through the vicious work of magicians Weyer both fostered skepticism and severely limited it.

This tightly bound Protestant adjustment of belief was some protection for Weyer against the dangerous charge that he was an atheist, a Sadducee, a Socinian heretic, or even a witch. Anyone who exposed Catholic "superstition" as he did was sure to win some Protestant approval by it; and anyone who so exposed Satan and black magic could scarcely be in the ranks of God's cosmic enemies or without faith in the worldly work of spirits. That Weyer shaded his true convictions for the sake of protective coloring is not necessarily so, but he certainly benefited with his fellow Protestants. He was skeptical about witchcraft, but by no means so about its foundation principle that some spirits and some men could and did act together in extreme defiance of God.

Aloof Skepticism

Oblique rejection of that principle came in the sixteenth century from such cultivated skeptics as Erasmus and Montaigne. Both did it largely by slighting the demonological controversy. In Erasmus's *The Praise of Folly* the speaker throughout is the allegorical Folly herself, who casually mocks charms, devils, astrology, alchemy, and magic. In his letters Erasmus seems to speak ironically of witchcraft. For the rest he simply "avoids every opportunity of encouraging the demonologists."[22] Montaigne has one essay that touches at moderate length on witchcraft. The witches in his neighborhood, he says, "are in mortal danger every time some new author comes along and attests to the reality of their visions. To apply examples that the Holy Writ offers us of such things, very certain and irrefragable examples, and bring them to bear on our modern events, requires greater ingenuity than ours, since we see neither their causes nor their means." We may believe God on such matters, but hardly men. To kill "we should have sharp and luminous evidence; and our life is too real and essential to vouch for these supernatural and fantastic accidents." We are excusable for "disbelieving a marvel . . . as long as we can turn aside and avoid the supernatural explanation by non-marvellous means." The arguments for the fact of witchcraft, Montaigne shrugs, he had not found to be compelling, though he does not try to disentangle "the proofs and reasons that are founded on experience and fact; . . . they have no end to take hold of; I often cut them as Alexander did his knot. After all, it is putting a very high price on one's conjectures to have a man roasted alive because of them."[23]

Montaigne and Erasmus did not approach demonology closely enough to grapple with the question of whether devils were active in the world, but the well-known Pietro Pomponazzi did. He decided that angels, either good or evil, did not exist. The idea of them was just a simplifying device by which sages of the past had tried to describe God's providence to uncomprehending masses. He acknowledged the occurrence of marvels but ascribed them all to psychological causes or to the action of the stars, which he thought God's conduit for managing earthly affairs. Unlike Montaigne, Pomponazzi did often try to untangle "proofs and reasons" based on "experience and facts," and in the course of it argued as deviously as any demonologist.[24]

Scot's Skepticism

Also an untangler of demonological proofs and reasons and a reinterpreter of experience and received "facts" was England's leading controversialist on witches, Reginald Scot. In his long book *The Discovery of Witchcraft* (1584),[25] he did not deny the existence of angels fallen and unfallen, but he did deny that they worked physically in the world of his time or that they ever had so worked except as God's messengers in such miracles as the Annunciation. Although Scot ironically acknowledged that some persons had the name of witches and that some claimed it, he denied that they ever achieved through magic any temporal contact with spirits, since, unless by miracle, finite spirits did not and could not act corporeally. All tales of wonders done by witches or magicians were lies, exaggerations, or misinterpretations. In the face of these "facts," thought Scot, prosecution for witchcraft was usually a miserable injustice grievously aggravated by cruel and panicky methods and by idiotic charges impossible either to establish or to resist. To credit the claims of any kind of magician was stupid gullibility. This last Scot did not press when he used Weyer, which he did extensively, gratefully, and respectfully—though never slavishly. Like Weyer, Scot was scornful of church magic, and, unlike him, also of lay ceremonial magic. Scot sympathized with those poor souls wrongly accused of selling themselves to devils, deprecated the delusions of those who honestly thought themselves to have closed such deals, and despised and exposed frauds.

Scot against papistry. Like Weyer's, Scot's use of militant Protestantism may have been largely self-protective. He went far beyond customary Protestant reticence on spirits, though not beyond Protestant spleen at "papistry," in arguing for a rationalistic interpretation of biblical testimony to spirit magic and to other demonic interventions in temporal affairs. The serpents that Pharaoh's magicians produced against Moses and Aaron and the apparition that the Witch of Endor showed Saul, Scot reduced to fraud or to natural events accommodated in statement to the understanding of the ancient Jewish populace and foolishly misread by commentators. Even the possessions in the New Testament he manfully declared to be illnesses and the exorcisms to be divine miracle. Men could not duplicate them without such empowerment as the Apostles received from Christ.

This exegesis was daring for a layman—even under Elizabeth's modestly tolerant regime; and Scot took more pains than Weyer had needed with his half-credulous stand to clear himself of suspicion that he had abandoned Christian faith in angels, the Trinity, and resurrection of the dead. From time to time Scot explicitly asserted faith in all, and he rebuked Sadducees and others who denied the personal existence of angels. He ended his long work with a weighty chapter to refute "Pneumatomachie," those who unlike him did deny every sort of separated spirit, including the divine. Scot insisted here not only on the Trinity but on angels and devils, and he tried to explain how finite spirits acted without physical manifestation to tempt men to sin or to support them against temptation.

Astrology and alchemy. Scot drew into his treatment of witchcraft a whole cluster of other occult practices that are related to witchcraft or used in it or, as he says of astrology and alchemy, have witchcraft hidden in them. He noticed prophecy, augury, divinatory dreams, "strange noises," and other oddities, and he treated skeptically the whole structure of demonology. His concern was to show how enormously varied and widespread these "arts" were, with their claims of cosmic connections and marvelous powers possible to men. He meant to discredit them all.

Scot's Credulous Foes

Sixteenth-century skeptics like Scot confronted an already vast and influential body of literature believing in witchcraft. Among both Catholics and Protestants perhaps the work on witches most attended over a long period was the *Malleus Maleficarum* ("Hammer of Witches") published a hundred years before Scot wrote by two Dominican Inquisitors, Heinrich Kramer (Institor in the Latinized version) and Jacob Sprenger. Their work was a massive handbook, chiefly for prosecutors, on witchcraft as a conspiratorial heresy inspired and managed from hell. They were in direct opposition to the celebrated *Canon Episcopi,* said to date from the fourth century and received in the Church through the fourteenth. Its thrust was that to believe in the marvels attributed to witches was itself a heresy. The *Malleus* was explicit and forthright that the heresy was the witchcraft, fully capable of most of the feats the *Canon* deprecated. The *Malleus* was credulous in the extreme about the worshipful relation of witches to devils and about the evil deeds they did in concert: pact, carnal intercourse, murder of unbaptized children, metamorphosis, and the like. It was also merciless in its prescriptions for detecting witches, wringing confessions from them, and killing them. Pope Innocent VIII had backed its authors in their efforts against the heresy. Between 1487 and 1520 fourteen editions of the *Malleus* appeared, and a modern authority says that a copy "lay on the bench of every judge, on the desk of every magistrate."[26] For Scot it was a bountiful provider of Rome-endorsed absurdities and horrors upon which to exclaim.

The chief living "witchmonger" (dealer in demonological superstitions) whom Scot wrote against was Jean Bodin, and the chief to write against Scot in the century was King James

VI of Scotland, soon to be James I of England. Both accused Weyer of being a witch, and James called Scot a Sadducee, one who in the path of the ancient sect denied the existence of spirits. Bodin was a man of great learning and intellectual power, much respected in England, and also of independent and offbeat opinions on spirits and on religion.[27] But he was wholly convinced of the existence, horrors, and dangers of witchcraft as conspiracy, and in his long *De la Demonomanie des Sorciers* (1580) he retailed most of the standard witchmongering tales and arguments about it. He had much legal experience with witches. King James, too, was a learned man, and as honest as his lights allowed. He was regally assertive and impatient of opposition in his brief *Daemonologie* (1597).[28] He had some investigative experience with witches, and, he thought, was once a target for their spells. In the middle of the seventeenth century a prominent Dutch witchmonger asserted that the king had had Scot's *Discovery* publicly burned. Modern authority inclines to accept the story.

Controversy after Scot

Scot saw very little published on his side of the controversy. A country rector, George Gifford, did write two brief treatises, the burden of which was that persons accused of *maleficia* were less likely to be associates of devils than to be their victims. The real guilt among witches, he insisted, belonged to the village "cunning men," so-called "good" or "white" witches, and to anyone who believed so strongly in witchcraft as to resort to them for counterwitchery. What Gifford offered, then, was an English parochial version of Weyer. Gifford defended accused witches as Weyer did on grounds of their ignorance and the impossibility of pact that would truly bind either witch or devil. He attacked cunning men much as Weyer did black magicians on grounds of their use of charms they knew to be attractive to devils. But Gifford had no notion of denying that devils could and did work in concert with men, though he reduced as much as he could the scope of the human power in the alliance.[29]

After Scot's death the controversy in England went briskly on for a hundred years, with the believers having much the

best of it in print, though gradually fading in influence, and
the unbelievers losing the argument when they handled it in
the old terms, even as they came to master the situation. A
mid-seventeenth-century dialectical rally for spirits from Cambridge Platonists and such Cabalistic mystagogues as Robert
Fludd earned much public respect but little abiding conviction.
Scot's reputation, meanwhile, grew in an anomalous way with
the republication of his work during the 1650s and 1660s. Probably many readers then admired him for his rationalism, but
still more for his detailed exposition of the sensational opinions
that he was resisting and for his salty retelling of marvelous
tales that he tried to discredit. For a long time few praised or
even noticed his fine conceptual feat of getting to the dubious
foundations of occult theory and hammering it consistently
throughout a very long and varied book. Scot's work endured
because he was as learned on occult matters as Robert Burton,
as rational on them as Francis Bacon and as consistent on the
evidence as Pomponazzi.

Chapter Two

Scot's Life and Works

We do not know enough about Reginald Scot's life to say for sure what experience of witches and witch trials may have moved him to write his monumental *Discovery of Witchcraft*. Perhaps, as one of his editors supposes, he did it hastily in 1583, moved by indignation about an infamous trial in Essex.[1] He published it the next year, apparently on his own responsibility, for it does not appear in the Stationers Register and so lacks the official recognition that entry there signifies. If Scot did publish boldly and impatiently, it indicated in him a state of moral arousal against legal abuse of witches, a state he could have come to in whole or in part by reading about the Chelmsford trials of 1582 in Essex or by personal investigation in 1581 of the charges against Margaret Simons at Rochester in northeastern Kent. The volume of his reading on witchcraft, though, indicates that he may have been into the literature long before those trials. But no detailed and positive evidence survives of what particular events may have set him to the study and to the writing of his astonishing book.

Scot's Family and Writings

Scot was born, probably in 1538, into an old, well-to-do, and locally influential family in Kent. The Scots did not belong to the nobility, but their holdings were sizable, and many of them served in Parliament and in various county offices. Reginald (the name appears often as Reynolde or Rainold) was the son, perhaps the only son, of Richard Scot, himself a younger son, and was named for his uncle Sir Reginald, who died in 1554 and was succeeded as head of the family by his son, Sir Thomas. To this very prominent and popular cousin, Reginald the witch writer was much indebted over the years.

Wood's *Athenae Oxonienses* says that the younger Reginald

went at seventeen to Hart College, Oxford, but left "without
the honor of a degree" and "settled at Smeeth, where he found
great incouragement in his studies from his kinsman Sir Thos.
Scot." Here Reginald married and "gave himself up solely to
solid reading, to the perusing of obscure authors that had by
the generality of Scholars been neglected, and at times of leisure
to husbandry and gardening, as it may partly appear from these
books following." The books as Wood lists them are:

*A Perfect Platform of a Hop-garden, and Necessary Instructions for
the Making and Maintenance Thereof, with Notes and Rules
for Reformation of All Abuses, &c.* London, 1576; the first
edition, however, was 1574;

*The Discovery of Witchcraft; Wherein the leud Dealing of Witches
and Witchmongers is Notably Detected, the Knavery of Conjurors,
the Impiety of Inchanters, the Folly of Southsayers, &c.* London,
1584; and

Discourse of Devils and Spirits (printed and bound together with
the *Discovery*).

Scot's activities.   That Scot's calling in life was not consistently that of a scholar or writer appears in such incidentally
acquired information, not all of it trustworthy, as that he was
a "Collector of subsidies to Q. Elizabeth in 15— for the county
of Kent" and that he acquired the title "armiger," esquire,
through having been a justice of the peace at some undetermined
time, probably between 1578 and 1584, and that he appears
as captain in the muster rolls of a force raised by his cousin
Sir Thomas against the Armada. Thomas Ady, also a writer
against witch persecutions, notices in his *A Candle in the Dark*
(1656) that Scot "was a student in the laws and learned in
the *Roman* Laws."[2] His name does not appear, though, in the
rolls of the Inner or Middle Temple or in those of Lincoln's
or Gray's Inn. He was a member of the Parliament of 1588–
89 for New Romney.

Scot on hop gardening.   Scot's active interest in hop raising suggests that in the early 1570s, anyway, he was much occu-
pied with the land, whether his own holdings or the far more
extensive ones of his cousin Sir Thomas. The book of fifty-odd
pages on hop gardening appears to have been a work of some

consequence for the cultivation of the hop in England. It went through three editions, the last in 1578 being "somewhat corrected and augmented," and seems to have been serviceable in breaking the monopoly for hops in the English market that Poppering in Flanders had long preserved by keeping the manner of cultivation secret. Scot's book strikes the modern reader (at least one ignorant of hop gardening) as impressively painstaking in both the text and the illustrative woodcuts. Scot may have gained some of his expertise by trial and error, but some also by penetrating Flemish secrecy, for his description of an "oast house" depends on knowledge of such a house at Poppering.[3]

Although Scot meant to instruct, his work is not without a touch of the spice that distinguishes his later book. The gardener will meet, he says, three kinds of hops: "the good and kindly Hoppe," "the unkindly Hoppe," and the "wylde Hoppe." The good one shows a great green stalk and a large, hard bell. But

the Hoppe that likes not his entertainment, namely his seate, his grounde, his keeper, his dunge or the manner of his setting, appeareth at the first out of the grounde greene and small in stalke, thick and tough in leaves, very like a nettle, which will be commonly devoured or much bytten with a little black flie.[4]

To protect the garden the cultivator may—arme everye hill with a few thornes, to defend them from the annoyance of Poultrie, which many times will scrape and bathe among the hylles and so discover and hurt the Springes, but a Goose is the most noysome vermine that can enter into this Garden . . . for a Goose will brut upon every yong . . . Hoppe budde . . . which will never growe afterwards, and therefore as well to avoide the Goose, as other noysome cattell, let your closure be made strong and kept tight. (14)

Speaking later of "divers men's follys," Scot warns that not "to cut excess roots" is "daungerous." Those who spare themselves that expense are "lyke unto them that refraigne to laye dung upon their corne lands, bicause they would not betraye it with so uncleanly a thing" (36). Scot's Epilogue sternly cites Ecclesiastes 13 and Proverbs 24 against the slothful.

Scot's vicissitudes. Although Scot inherited some property from his father and in 1575 a "moiety" from his aunt, Lady Winifred Rainford, he may well have lost it all, for he says in dedicating *The Discovery* partly to his cousin Sir Thomas: "My foot being under your table, my hand in your dish, or rather in your purse." At another place he mentions ruefully that "to have a ship, and to let hir lie always in the docke: which thing how profitable it is, I can say somewhat by experience." His will, too, seems to testify to his losses. Written on September 15, 1599, just before his death, it says of his second wife, "whome yf I had not matched withal I had not dyed worth one groat" (Nicholson, xxviii).

Scot apparently had no immediate family except for his first wife, Jane Cobbe, of old yeoman descent, and their daughter, Elizabeth, and his second wife, Alice, who brought him some property, and her daughter, Marie Collyer. Whether Collyer was the stepdaughter's maiden or married name is unknown, nor do we have her mother's family or first married name. Scot's first marriage seems to have been in 1554 and the second about 1584.

The London printer of the *Hop Garden* laments in a note the author's inability to be at hand to advise him during the book's production. Biographers have inferred that Scot may for a while at least have been bound to the country by duties as his Cousin Thomas's "man of business" or perhaps by the need to attend his aunt Winifred, who was declared insane in 1572. Whether Sir Thomas financed or otherwise assisted in publication of either of Reginald's books we have no notion.

Scot's Kent

The southeast of England, in which Scot apparently spent his whole life, was perhaps the most "advanced" part of the country, and Scot's own county of Kent was one of England's most prosperous and democratic. The southern counties had comparatively efficient administration and records, enabling historians now to decide with some confidence that in the second half of the sixteenth century they were England's most thickly populated. To judge by the muster rolls of the Armada year, 1588, Gloucester, Somerset, Kent, and Devon together set in arms over ten thousand men between the ages of sixteen and sixty, far more than other counties seem to have provided.[5]

Kent's geography was commercially advantageous. The Cinque Ports ranged along its eastern coast, the closest of all English harbors to the rich and cultivated Low Countries. The lower Thames was Kent's northern border, and London was close at hand so that much of the city's food supply came from Kent, which its contemporary historian, William Lambarde, fondly called the "garden of England." It had, he explained, a great many parks and orchards, though half of the deer parks had been turned to tillage during Elizabeth's reign. Its proximity to the Low Countries, where agriculture was most knowingly practiced, was a help in improving cultivation in Kent, as Scot's publication on hop gardening demonstrates. It was one of several treatises on farming in southern England, including one on horse breeding by Sir Thomas Scot (Nicholson, xv). How serious the Scots and others were about such progressive studies appears in Reginald's commendation of his own book as "a recompense to the labourer, as a commodity to the housekeeper, as a comfort to the poor and as a benefit to the country or common-wealth. . . ."[6]

Lambarde notices that the gentry of Kent are not of such old stock as some other counties could show, for "new men"— merchants, lawyers, and low-ranked courtiers—often chose to move from London into Kent. This did not reduce the Kentish-man's pride in his county and in its nobility, though,[7] and it did, apparently, in informed and thoughtful opinion improve the population mix. Thomas Fuller is among those who praise England for its yeomanry, a propertied class of sturdy independent farmers far more serviceable to the state than such an oppressed peasantry as predominated in France. Lambarde says that "a man may find sundry yeomen although otherwise for wealth comparable with the gentle sort that will not yet for all that change their condition, nor desire to be apparelled with the titles of gentry."[8] The Scots, though gentry, may have had more in common with Kent's yeomen than with its nobility.

The Work of Justices

The Scots were, nevertheless, presumably superior to the yeo-men in education and in public service. Particularly they served (Reginald perhaps among them) as justices of the peace, and

for this office and for the protection of their own interests they
needed some knowledge of the law, as Reginald presumably
had, whether or not they went the full progress through the
Inns of Court, as he apparently did not. The J.P. (not paid
for his onerous labors)[9] became a very important functionary
for local government in Elizabeth's England. His duties and
responsibilities Lambarde laid forth in a book on the office that
applies especially to Kent. Most pressingly, the J.P. was to protect the people from force and violence, which were abuses
exceedingly frequent even in "civilized" Kent. He applied the
laws that controlled labor and those on attendance at church.
He was to deal fairly with the poor and to accept no bribes.
He was a sworn believer in the established government, having
taken the oath of Royal Supremacy. He had authority to check
rioters, to decide between the claims of master and servant,
and to suppress illegal hunting. He could send men to jail for
disregard of the statute of liveries or that of musters, or for
misusing export licenses. And, of course, he had authority in
cases of witchcraft, conjuring, or objectionable prophesying.

The weightier decisions the J.P. usually handed down at
"quarter sessions," when he met with his fellows from all over
the county. They sustained each other with joint wisdom. At
these sessions indictments were returned, juries assembled, cases
tried, and judgments delivered. The disqualification of Catholics
reduced the size of such J.P. sessions and tempered the disposition of courts in Scot's time.[10]

In all sessions the court machinery was crude for such services
as the bringing of witnesses and exhibits and the discounting
of public opinion. Justice was likely to be quick and rough; it
might very well miscarry, and not only in witchcraft cases.[11]
On the whole, though, the common man seems to have had
more show against his betters than in most countries of the
Continent; and the poor, including witch types, had the benefit,
though rather a miserable one, of laws for their maintenance
at the expense of the county. Destitute elderly husbandmen
set adrift by enclosure, mustered out soldiers and sailors, and,
of course, old women who appeared to be witches might all
get some relief by applying to J.P.s.[12]

However overconfidently slapdash the procedures of the J.P.
court may seem to us and however barbarous some of its punish-

ments, it did rest on a conception of law promptly administered without regard for privilege and with regard for evidence and for the rights of the accused as well as the public weal. The possibility and even the likelihood of bad performance in such courts are manifest. The queen often complained of the incompetence of J.P.s.[13] But the intent of the law was basically sound, and the interpretation of it by those responsible for applying it must often have been a very honest one.

The Scots and Witch Trials

Reginald Scot had strong and elevated ideas of the treatment that an accused witch was entitled to from the courts of England. The judge's part, he says in dedicating the *Discovery* first to a "Lord cheefe Baron of hir Majesties Court," is to "here with courtesie, and to determine with equitie; it cannot but be apparent unto you, that when punishment exceedeth the fault, it is rather to be thought vengeance than correction" (vii). Scot did not directly attack either the laws on witchcraft or the magistrates, and in fact in chapter 8 of Book I he speaks of the "excellent magistrates" who serve the queen (13), and when he listed for his cousin Sir Thomas the justifications for his book that he hoped would procure it consideration, he named not only the "law of God, the law of nature" and the "rule of reason" but the "law of this land." He was unquestionably discontented, though, with that law's operation in many cases. "See . . . whether the evidence be not frivolous, & . . . the proof . . . incredible, . . . ghesses, presumptions, & impossibilities contrarie to reason, scripture, and nature. See also what persons complaine upon [witches] . . . whether they be not of the basest, the unwisest, & and most faithless kind of people. Also . . . waie what accusations and crimes they laie to their charge. . . . Note also how easilie [the accused] may be brought confesse that which they never did, nor lieth in the power of man to do" (Epistle, xiii–iv).

That without any known local outcry Scot could thus impugn English justice for witches may be some slim indication of how little infected parts of England were by the miasma of witch persecutions. The comparative paucity of witch cases in the sensibly run county of Kent and the general good sense of its thriving

and nicely proportioned population perhaps allowed some deliberate application of the *Discovery*'s prescriptions. Sir Thomas
Scot was Deputy Lieutenant of the Shire, empowered to sit as
a J.P. "I see," says Reginald to him in the epistle, "among
other malefactors manie poore old women convented before
you for working of miracles, otherwise called witchcraft, and
therefore I thought you also a meet person to whom I might
commend my book" (xiii). The implication that Sir Thomas
had in fact rightly conducted sessions on witch cases seems rather
a hesitant one. But perhaps his fondness for Reginald did per-
suade him to restrict the persecution in Kent and to sponsor
the book with his local influence, which the queen once irritably
declared exceeded her own.

Some Witch Cases

Kent was not so free of witch inquiries and trials in the 1580s
that Scot could not attend some within its borders, nor was it
geographically remote from another county that thought itself
especially plagued by witches—Essex, just across the Thames
to the north. In the *Discovery,* however, Scot in treating affairs
personally known to him speaks only of Kentish ones. He did
not, apparently, attend the examination of the St. Osyth witches
and their famous trial at Chelmsford, Essex, in 1582, which
some historians claim inspired his treatise. He seems to have
known it chiefly from the pamphlet literature.

Scot did certainly do his best to acquire personal experience
concerning witchcraft and the occult in general. He attended
trials and followed up cases; he talked to court officials, to towns-
men, and to the accused; he corresponded with practicing magicians; he consulted kinsmen in divine orders about biblical
passages; and apparently he tried to infiltrate witch organizations
(but could find none) and to be initiated as a witch (but was
never accepted).

The case of Margaret Simons.   In the *Discovery* the case
most informative for Scot's biography is one dealt with in his
first few pages—that of the "assizes holden at Rochester, Anno
1581." Margaret Simons was arraigned for witchcraft, says Scot,
"at the instigation and complaint of divers fond and malicious
persons; and especiallie by the means of one *John Ferrall* vicar

of that parish: with whom I talked about that matter and found him both fondlie assotted in the cause and enviouslie bent towards hir: and (which is worse) as unable to make a good account of his faith, as she whom he accused."

The vicar's son, "an ungratious boie," had passed the woman's house and so resented her dog's barking at him as to draw his knife and chase the dog to her door, where she "rebuked him with some such words as the boie disdained." In about a week he sickened. The vicar "(who thought himselfe so privileged, as he little mistrusted that God would visit his children with sickness)" decided, "partlie (as he himselfe told me) by the relation of other witches, that his sonne was by hir bewitched. Yea, he also told me, that this his sonne (being as it were past all cure) received perfect health at the hands of another witch" (4).

The vicar charged also that when he most wanted to read distinctly to his congregation his voice failed him, "which hee could impute, he said, to nothing else, but to hir inchantment. When I advertised the poore woman hereof . . . she told me that his voice did much faile. . . . But, sir, said she, you shall understand that this our vicar is diseased with such a kind of hoarsenesse, as divers of our neighbours in this parish . . . doubted that he had the French pox . . . untill such time as . . . he had brought from *London* a certificate under the hands of two physicians, that his horaseness proceeded from a disease in the lungs. Which certificate he published in the church in the presence of the whole congregation. . . . And this I know to be true by the relation of divers honest men of that parish."

"If one of the Jurie had not beene wiser than the others," Scot concludes, "she had beene condemned thereupon, and upon other as ridiculous matters. . . . For the name of witch is so odious, and her power so feared among the common people, that if the honestest bodie living chance to be arraigned thereupon, she shall hardlie escape condemnation" (5).

This first account of a case that Scot looked into personally is characteristic. He excludes all hint of mystery and equally all hint of special authority and learning about occult powers on his part or anyone else's. Whereas John Dee showed fascination with mysterious "knocking and rapping" in the night, and the influential Calvinist preacher William Perkins[14] wrote on witches always with the authority of a learned pneumatologist, Scot's interest is in the ordinary and the readily explicable, and his authority is that of personal investigation and good sense. Did the woman have real power to smite the vicar and his son? The question was too fantastic for Scot to bother with in the face of commonplace explanations that surfaced with commonsense inquiry. To fathom the matter needed no pneumatological lore, only a few questions asked about town.

So Scot finishes with a stout indictment of the court itself. The system did work, but only barely so. One juror showed some sense. The absurd charges and the weak evidence were themselves display enough to expose the foolishness and injustice of the whole mindset that allowed criminal accusations of witchcraft. Much later in his book Scot says that ". . . it is ridiculous (as Pomponacius saith) to leave manifest things and such as by natural reason may be proved, to seeke unknowne things, which by no likelihood can be conceived, nor tried by anie rule of reason" (114). Scot cared little about the windings of metaphysics upon which the witchmongers relied. He argued in any way that he could—largely with down-to-earth irony—for proper legal procedure to insure that witches had such justice as the legal system could provide in any sort of criminal case.

The case of Davie's wife. In the second example personally known to him of the devil in Kent, Scot has the same concerns as in the first and the same manner of expressing them. He tells the story of a woman's hallucination. The wife of Simon Davie was "pensive and sad" and then "grew . . . to some perturbation of mind . . . and secret lamentation." Simon "could not but demand the cause of hir . . . moorning" until finally she fell on her knees and "told him that she had (contrarie to God's lawe) & to the offense of all good christians, to the injurie of him, and speciallie to the loss of hir owne soule, bargained and given hir soule to the divell, to be delivered unto him within a short space." The good man comforted her with insistence that her deal was "void and of none effect," for Christ had already bought her soul. She wept then that she had bewitched him and their children, to which he replied: "Be content . . . Christ shall unwitch us." And this, says Scot, "I knowe is true."

When the "time approached that the divell should . . . take

. . . the woman" they watched and prayed "and suddenlie about midnight there was a great rumbling beelowe under his chamber windowe, which amazed them exceedinglie. For they conceived, that the divell was beelowe, though he had no power to come up, bicause of their praiers." Now, says Scot,

He that noteth this womans . . . confession, freelie and voluntarilie made, how everie thing concurred that might serve to adde credit thereunto, and yeeld matter for hir condemnation, would not think but that if *Bodin* were foreman of hir inquest, he would crie: Guiltie: & would hasten execution upon hir; who would have said as much before any judge in the world, if she had benne examined; and have confessed no lesse if she had beene arraigned thereupon. But God knoeth, she was innocent of anie of these crimes: howbeit she was brought lowe and pressed downe with the weight of this humor, so as both hir rest and sleepe were taken awaie . . . and her fansies troubled and disquieted with despaire. . . . And yet I beleeve, if any mishap had insued to her husband, or his children; few witchmongers would have had it otherwise but that she had bewitched them. And she . . . so constantlie persuaded hir selfe to be a witch, that she judged hir selfe worthie of death; insomuch as being reteined in hir chamber, she sawe not anie one carrieng a faggot to the fier, but she would saie it was to make a fier to burne hir for witcherie. But God knoweth she had bewitched none, neither insued there anie hurt unto anie, by hir imagination, but unto hir selfe.

And then, reverting to a question that he had made big in his reader's mind, Scot gave the slyly postponed answer: "as for the rumbling, it was by occasion of a sheepe, which was flawed, and hong by the wals, so as a dog came and devoured it; whereby grew the noise which I before mentioned: and she being now recovered, remaineth a right honest woman, far from such impietie, and ashamed of hir imaginations, which she perceiveth to have growne through melancholie" (43–44).

The Pythoness of Westwell. Among his sixteen chapters on "Pythonists" (those supposed to prophesy or be clairvoyant through a familiar spirit) Scot has a "true storie of a wench practising hir diabolical witchcraft, and ventriloquie An. 1574. at *Westwell* in *Kent,* within six miles where I dwell" (101). One day in October the servant girl Mildred "was possessed with sathan," and to her help came "twoo ministers and preachers of Gods word." They wrestled a day with the demon and got from him that he had been sent into the maid by "old *Alice*" of Westwell, who had kept him for twenty years in two bottles behind her house. He named three persons that he had killed for her. The preachers ordered him to go, but "he went not," and then, after more wrestling, did so. Everyone prayed in thankfulness, and "noting this in a peece of paper," they departed. "Sathans voice did differ much from the maids voice, and all that he spake was in his owne name" (102–3).

Scot was not himself present for this bout with Satan, but he quotes largely from a deposition by the two clergymen and several other persons including the householder for whom the possessed maid worked. How, then, he asks, did "mother Alice escape condemnation and hanging, being arraigned upon this evidence?" Well, before two wise justices the maid was exposed as a ventriloquist, and the two ministers who exorcised her devil as full of enmity to Mother Alice. So now, says Scot, "compare this wench with the Witch of Endor (I Samuel:28) & you shall see that both cousenages may be doone by one art" (105).

Scot's Minor Contacts

Scot has many other and briefer accounts of contacts that show his personal interest and inquiry. In his chapter on theurgy ("high" magic) he inserts a letter "sent unto me, by one which at this present time lieth as a prisoner condemned in the king's bench" for practicing magic "and reprieved by hir majesties mercie." The letter came to Scot at his request from "T. E. Maister of art, and practiser both of physicke, and also in times past, of certaine vaine sciences . . . wherein he openeth the truth touching these deceits" (393). In the letter T. E. expresses intense regret for the years that he spent working at magic without ever finding "anie matter of truth to be doone in those wicked sciences, but onlie meere cousenings and illusions." He recommends to Scot a "booke, written in the old Saxon toong, by one, Sir John Manborne, a divine of Oxenford, three hundred yeares past; wherein he openeth all the illusions & inventions of those arts and sciences." T. E. "left the booke with a parson of Slangham in Sussex, where if you send for it in my name, you may have it." The recommendation of this work was, it seems, in quittance of a promise that T. E. could not keep "except I had the better warrant from my L. of Leicester" to discuss magic with Scot in detail. Scot did zealously send to the parson for the book, but, he tells us with pique, that "such is his follie and superstition that . . . he would not lend it" (395).

Scot knew personally, too, a fraud and criminal who conjured under one name and juggled under another and "everie way was a cousener: his qualities and feats were to me and manie other well knowne and detected. And yet the opinion conceived of him was most strange and wonderful." To think of this man, Scot says, grieves him "bicause his knaverie and cousenage reached to the shedding of innocent bloud" (116). Scot knew also a witch who drowned himself when he "could not prevaile to be accepted as a sufficient witness against himselfe." Such deranged acts, Scot indicates, are the sort of thing to be expected of those who make spontaneous confessions of witchcraft, and even Bodin and the *Malleus Maleficarum* record such suicides (38).

Since Bodin asserted that witches swear to the devil to recruit others into witchery and that they do, the tale goes, bring in about fifty apiece, Scot tried (seriously, it would seem) to be solicited. "I have made triall, as also of the residue of their coosening devices; and have been with the best, or rather the woorst of them, to see what might be gathered out of their counsels; and have cunninglie treated with them thereabouts: and further, have sent certaine old persons to indent with them, to be admitted into their societie. But as well by their excuses and delaies, as by other circumstances, I have tried and found all their trade to be a meare coosening" (37).

Scot and the Literature

Though beyond any question Scot investigated witchcraft at first hand as far as he possibly could and was able here and there in the *Discovery* to testify to personal experiences of witchmongering foolishness, most of his knowledge of it had to come from books. He seems to have read everything he could get hold of, both authors in favor of prosecuting witches and those doubtful about it. The latter were in short supply and were often hidden in works with other interests; Scot seems to have searched for them all. What he found he used with diligence and discretion, and much of it in detail.

An English pamphlet. His reading had to be mostly Continental because there was so little in English. But Scot was able to criticize the pamphlet on the St. Osyth case and through it English publication in general. "As touching the opinion of our writers therein in our own age; yea in our owne countrie, you shall see it doth not onlie agree with forren cruelty but surmounteth it farr. If you read a foolish pamphlet dedicated to the Lord *Darcy* by W.W. 1582. you shall see that he affirmeth, that all those tortures are farre too light, and their rigor too mild; and that in that respect he impudentlie exclameth against our magistrates, who suffer them to be but hanged, when murtherers, & such malefactors be so used, which deserve not the hundredth part of their punishment" (13).

Scot was scornful of the pamphlet, and was apparently convinced, as modern historians are, that the Lord Darcy to whom it was dedicated and the listed author, W.W., were one and the same—the J.P. who heard the case. In the *Discourse of Devils and Spirits* Scot says:

Now how *Brian Darcies* he spirits and shee spirits, Tittie and Tiffin, Suckin and Pidgin, Liard and Robin, &c.: his white spirits and blacke spirits, graie spirits and red spirits, divell tode and divell lambe, divels cat and divels dam, . . . can stand consonant with the word of GOD, or true philosophie, let heaven and earth judge. In the mean time, let anie man with good consideration peruse that booke published by W.W. and it shall suffice to satisfie him in all that may be required touching the vanities of the witches examinations, confessions, and executions: where, though the tale be told onlie of the accusers part, without anie other answer of theirs than their adversaries setteth downe; mine assertions will be sufficientlie prooved true. I will saie no more for the confutation thereof, but referre you to the booke itself; whereto if nothing be added that may make to their reproch, I dare warrent nothing is left out that may serve to their condemnation. See whether the witnesses be not single of what credit, sex and age they are; namelie lewd, miserable, and envious poore people; most of them which speake to anie purpose being old women, & children of the age of 4.5.6.7.8 or 9. yeares.

And note how and what the witches confesse, and see of what weights and importance the causes are; whether their confessions be not woone through hope of favour, and extorted by flatterie or threats, without proofe. But in so much as there were not past seventeene or eighteene condemned . . . I will say the lesse. . . . (455)

Scot's strictures against living fellow subjects of the queen were hardly less severe than those against dead Catholic foreigners. **Continental works.** The fact is, of course, that the Darcy pamphlet, as prominent a publication by an Englishman against witches as was contemporary to Scot's writing, was trivial compared with the Continental works that Scot cites and rages against—the *Malleus Maleficarum* and Bodin's *De la Demonomanie des Sorciers* chief among them. Scot apparently had no personal acquaintance or correspondence with any of those whose books he attacks. Bodin had visited England with Queen Elizabeth's suitor, the duke of Alençon, in 1579, and had met the occultist John Dee and Samuel Harsnett, who later wrote a skeptical book on demonic possession in which he praises Bodin's work before the *Demonomanie*.[15] But Scot was, of course, never of the court. He says, "What Bodin is, I knowe not, otherwise than by report; . . . and this man (as I understand) by profession is a civill lawier" (36). Scot seems never to have been out of England and to have had no correspondence with any Continental writer on witchcraft.

With his assaults on Bodin, the *Malleus,* Lambert Daneau, and others, Scot entered (as most English writers on witches did not) directly into the international controversy. He has ten or twelve lines against Continentals for one against Britons. The *Discovery* is, in fact, one of the most comprehensive works on the occult to be published in the sixteenth and seventeenth centuries, and for more than one hundred years it had, as most English books of the kind did not, a growing currency abroad. A Dutch translation of 1609 was twice reprinted.

On Astrology and Alchemy

Of the occult practices auxiliary to magic that Scot treats, the two most developed and most widely known were astrology and alchemy. He does not seem as familiar with their literature as with that of demonology. He treats it, though, with his usual searing scorn, leaving almost unmentioned not only the ancient dignity of the studies but their elaborate rationales. He concentrated on the absurdity of their grand purposes and claims compared to their feeble achievements, thus displaying their fraudulence.

Scot has no local tales of astrologers, but he does tell of a Kentish yeoman on whom a prestidigitator claiming to be an alchemist played a confidence game (297 ff.). Whether Scot knew the luckless farmer personally he does not say. The brief Book XIV, which he gives to alchemy, is mostly such stories, with the Canon's Yeoman's Tale figuring prominently. Astrology he handles in connection with the "Art of Conjuration," which makes great use of astrological signs and forces, and of "Augurie," of which astrology is a principal division. He cites briefly some simple and highly rational criticisms of astrology that are close kin to those we may hear today,[16] as that "there be in the heavens diverse movings as yet to men unknowne . . . starres and bodies . . . which cannot be seene, either through their exceeding highnes, or that hitherto are not tried with anie observation of the art" (169).

On "Juggling" and Natural Magic

Two pursuits related to spirit magic but comparatively innocent of the faults that Scot charged it with are prestidigitation and "natural magic." The first Scot treats at some length because although not in itself blasphemous or fraudulent, it was useful to blasphemous frauds in firming up their dupes' deluded faith in spirit magic. Natural magic, too, could be thus misused, and it had a tendency to slide over into an objectionable spirit magic.

The dozen chapters that Scot gave to natural magic have exposed him to some deprecatory modern comment. Thus the *Dictionary of National Biography* (1963) says sadly that he "fell victim to contemporary superstition in his references to medicine and astrology," as though his cautious expression of the opinion of "curious [natural] magicians" that "stones receive their vertues . . . of the planets and heavenlie bodies" (242) were equivalent to full faith in werewolves and flights to the Sabbat. One might as well charge the great nineteenth-century physicist, Sir Oliver Lodge, with superstition for his declared belief in the ether and for his long use of it for various descriptions in macrophysics. Scot had no more means to know for sure how stones got their "vertues" than Sir Oliver had to know how light traveled through the universe. And besides, Scot was admittedly out of his element and simply declaring a general confidence in what we would now call *science*. He rightly felt a need to distinguish its entirely legitimate marvels from those illegitimate ones ascribed to witches. He notices that "these notable and wonderfull experiments and conclusions that are found out in nature itself" can be made offensive if "deceipt and illusion is annexed thereunto." If whatever "we cannot comprehend" we consider supernatural, then a "witch, a papist, a conjuror, a counsener, and a juggler may make us beleeve they are gods" (254).

Scot then passes to something easier to judge than natural magic, something in which he was evidently more at home. Prestidigitation was like hop gardening, a plain matter, easily learned and susceptible of picturization. The *Discovery* has four neat drawings very like those in the earlier book. They show trick knives and bodkins and a table for a beheading act. The text retails more than fifty specific illusions with balls, coins, paper, cards, handkerchiefs, boxes, threads, knives, and rings. He could go on indefinitely, he says, but hopes that he has delivered the principles of this "art of juggling." And "so long as the power of almightie God is not transposed to the juggler, . . . so long as the juggler confesse in the end that these are no supernatural actions," the tricks will "not onlye be found among indifferent actions, but such as greatlie advance the power and glorie of God, discovering their pride and falsehood that take upon them to worke miracles" (288–89). Scot never relaxes his main purpose: to explode the pretensions of so-called magicians.

Scot's *Discovery* Described

The first edition of the *Discovery* runs to 488 pages and has the seventy-two-page *Discourse of Devils and Spirits* added. It has a list of 214 "forren authors used" as well as twenty-three who are English. The foreigners include Homer, Socrates, Plato, and Aristotle; Apuleius and Plutarch; Plotinus, Porphyry, Proclus, and Iamblichus and Marsilio Ficino, their Renaissance translator; Albertus Magnus, Aquinas, and Duns Scotus; eight rabbis; and a score of sixteenth-century demonologists, of whom Agrippa, Weyer, Daneau, Jerome Cardan, and Bodin get most attention. Among skeptics Scot names Pomponazzi and also Cicero, to whom he was indebted on divination. He seems to have read Latin well, although he depends on others for translations of verse. Throughout the work numerous marginal notes inform us of Scot's debts. At the end is an elaborate table of contents. "The summe of everie chapter conteined in the sixteene books of this discoverie, with discourse of divels and spirits annexed thereunto." The chapters number about 250, most of them brief; and mixed with them in the later books are nearly thirty "charmes," usually with headings of their own and running, many of them, to a page or more.

In the first five books Scot explains "who they are that are called witches"; "what charges, testimonies and witnesses are allowed" against them; the accusation of a "bargaine with the divel," and how hollow it is; "witchmongers opinions concerning evill spirits" with confutations and a treatment of "transformations" of men into animals. From the sixth book through the fifteenth (with a brief digression in the eighth book on the cessation of miracles) Scot concerns himself with the meaning of some Hebrew words upon whose traditional reading his foes depend for biblical authority against witches. For his readings of the Hebrew, Scot is heavily indebted to Weyer. For that part of his treatment of such words as has to do with magic Scot apparently takes specimen "charmes" and incantations from a manuscript copy of a work of magic known as the *Lemegeton or Lesser Key of Solomon*. He uses also its catalog of demon princes. His list of them resembles closely that in Weyer's *Pseudomonarchia Daemonum*, which seems, like the *Discovery*, to be from the first book of the *Lemegeton*.[17]

Scot's *Discourse* has thirty-four chapters of which the first is "of philosphers opinions, also the manner of their reasoning here upon, and the same confuted." The second chapter is Scot's "own opinion concerning this argument, to the disproofe of some writers hereupon." To these two chapters Scot gives only a rather presumptuous three pages, ticking off "Sadducees and Peripateticks" as "ungodlie and profane"; "Plato, Proclus, Plotinus, Porphyrie" as "fond and superstituous"; "Psellus, Nider,

Sprenger . . . Bodin . . . Iamblichus, &c" as "vaine & absurd." He passes then to individual attacks on them and on such others as Dionysius the Areopagite and "Cabalists, Talmudists, and Schoolmen." From the twelfth chapter he concentrates again upon his own opinion. The courageous heart of that opinion is "That divels assaults are spiritual and not temporall." This article of his belief was the key to his entire resistance to the feasibility of witchcraft as wonder-working.

Scot's References

Scot's principal modern editor asserted that Scot hurried the composition of the *Discovery* or, at least, the printing of it.[18] Whether or not he was right (the errors he points to seem few and trivial considering the size and complexity of the work), the *Discovery* is not wholly trustworthy in its marginal notes or in its reports on the statements of some of Scot's foes. Of the first twenty-five references to the *Malleus,* for instance, four are faulty in the number they give for question or chapter. About an equal proportion of references to Bodin's *Demonomanie* are misleading in chapter reference. But for most of these, the material that Scot refers to may be found somewhere in the works he names. Considering the very great number of marginal references, the flaws in them are not nearly enough to shake our faith in Scot's knowledge of his authors.

Occasionally Scot misreads or slightly distorts what opponents have said. For instance, in retelling from the *Malleus* a story of devil-originated impotence, Scot calls its hero, by no means celibate, "a yoong priest" (61), whereas his source says just "young man."[19] Similarly, in reciting "some of *Monsieur Bodins* lies" Scot gives as one that at their "magicall assemblies the witches never faile to danse; and in their danse they sing these; Har har, divell, divell, danse here, danse here, plaie here, plaie here, Sabbath sabbath." They brought "out of Italie into Fraunce, that danse, which is called La volta" (32). In the place in the *Demonomanie* that Scot cites, Bodin does indeed say that "Sorciers" brought "la volte" with its insolent and impudent movements from Italy, but the rest of the "lie" that Scot ascribes to him is missing.[20] Scot does Bodin an injustice too in claiming that he "mainten-

eth for true the most part of Ovid's *Metamorphosis* . . . : marie
he thinketh that some one tale therein may be false" (73). What
Bodin actually said was that he passes over Ovid because he
meddles with the truth in several fables, though one tale, that
on Lycaon, is not wholly incredible.[21] Assailing the *Malleus*
again, Scot maintains that it insists "holie water maie not be
sprinkled upon bewitched beasts, but must be powered into
their mouths" (229). The *Malleus* had in fact named such pour-
ing among "unlawful remedies . . . superstitious . . .
actions."[22]

But again the number of faults of the kind in Scot's work is
not nearly large enough, compared with the number of sound
uses, to cast doubt upon his honesty or to invalidate his general
case against the witchmongers. Whether we now read them
or Scot on them, they will mostly seem to us about as misled
and misleading as he says.

Scot's Soundness

Many modern writers have praised Scot for being ahead of
his time, and about as many have added that he was not as
far ahead as he ought to have been, since he did not deny
the existence of either witches or devils. The fact is, however,
that Scot went quite as far against witches and devils as the
logic of his case demanded and the need for public impact allowed. He did have a real effect, it seems, upon public opinion
about witches (at any rate some of his successors in the struggle
thought so)[23] both in England and elsewhere. If like Pomponazzi, Socinus, and others who insisted that demons were myth
or metaphor he had opened himself fully to the charge of being
a "Sadduccee" or "atheist," he must have forfeited most of
what influence he could hope for. Sir Isaac Newton could say
that spirits were "mere desires of the mind,"[24] but it would
not have done for Scot even if he had believed it—which he
did not.

Chapter Three

Scot Ahead of His Time

A few years ago the two most noticed living writers in English on sixteenth-century witchcraft were Montague Summers, proclaiming with horror and learning all the traditional abominations, and Margaret Murray, denying most of the tradition in favor of her theory that witchcraft was a surviving nature cult erroneously thought Satanic. Summers's views were substantially those of the witchmongers Scot wrote against, and Murray's are now thought ill-founded, however influential among our contemporary witches. In amendment of Murray and Summers later authorities offer conjectures and conclusions that have indeed altered the picture of the craft and of its persecution. Some of these opinions now prevalent among professional historians and anthropologists Reginald Scot had set out four hundred years ago, and others he had resisted.

Modern Opinion on Witchcraft

The most positive and sweeping new opinions on European witchcraft are those of British historian Norman Cohn. He insists that the notion of a Satanic cult is fantasy created mostly in the imaginations of Inquisitors who could and did use torture to get it confirmed by their helpless victims.[1] Many of the stereotypes of cult evil (cannibalism; orgies; obscene worship; ritual murder, particularly of children) the pagan world had charged against early Christians. Cathars, too, and other medieval heretics—often identified with witches—were thought to worship Satan with obscene caresses, baby-killing and eating, and general orgies of the sort to which witches were made to confess. Such duplication of charges through the centuries suggests to Cohn that they were always without merit except in the cultivated fears and repressed desires of the accusers. The accusations were the vile work of "Europe's inner demons," part of a general psychosis.

Traditional views attacked. How explain the great rationalistic articulation of orthodox doctrine on witchcraft, much of it based on the work of St. Augustine and St. Thomas Aquinas? It was by egregious misreading of them, says Cohn, for they spoke not of witches but of ceremonial magicians, whom they slandered by calling them allies of Satan. The magician was learned, ambitious, and reckless enough to try to benefit himself by contact with spirits. But his efforts were very different from those ascribed to witches. The Thomistic articulation of doctrine on magic concerned almost exclusively "conjuration of demons" by use of language, apparatus, and rite. The Church did magicians an injustice in holding their spirit-summoning to be demonolatry. "Nowhere in the surviving books of magic is there a hint of Satanism" or any suggestion "that the magician should ally himself with the demonic hosts, or do evil to win the favor of the Prince of Evil. Not a word is said about reversing or profaning religious rituals or observances. . . . The demons are not supposed to be worshipped but . . . mastered and commanded . . . through the power of God who created all spirits . . . as well as all human beings."[2]

Thomists denied, however, that any sort of magic could give its practitioner real control of demons. All deliberate contacts were by agreement, either tacit or express, conveyed to the devil in the magician's conjuration. This piously partisan insistence, Cohn seems to say, provided a bridge, the demonic pact, to link magicians with witches as demon worshipers. And thus orthodoxy gradually identified them, although the witch used little or no ceremony so that any pact he made with the devil had to be direct and explicit. Furthermore, Cohn claims, nowhere in the rationale of magic, whether the medieval Church's or the thaumaturge's own, do we find the slightest suggestion that the ceremonialists were a sect or engaged in hellish conspiracy.[3]

Magic's profanations. Cohn concedes that surviving incantations do call for prayer and sacrifice to demons and for the use of holy names, including the Hebrew names for God. He does not seem to consider, as Montague Summers did, that such usage is self-evidently that very "reversing or profaning" of "religious rituals" that Cohn had denied magic hints at. Since the usage implies that the magician coerces not only subordinate spirits but their Creator, it may seem to any religious person to be profanation enough. Just as in Huysman's *La Bas* the renegade priest officiating at a Black Mass blasphemously professes to compel Christ by the rites of consecration of bread and wine, so did earlier magicians seek to do it by their ceremonies. And most assuredly those who used goetical rites (one of which, strangely, Cohn prints to exhibit the magician's piety)[4] are a contrary sort of Christianity. Granted that defenders like Agrippa of theurgical procedures tried honestly to put on them the pious face that Cohn claims for all. But as appears in, for instance, Marlowe's *Dr. Faustus,* black magicians could well be thought one with witches as servants of Satan, except in the manner and scale of their magical pretensions.[5] The Thomistic account of magic easily covered them both, though it did lack such items of the developed witch doctrine as the Sabbat and the coven. And the Thomistic articulation is not fantastic—except, of course, as any exposition of contacts with totally unmanifest spiritual beings is. Magicians and their infamous practices did exist, and St. Thomas did give a solid, if wholly conceptual, account of them and of the spirits they sought to use.[6]

The "impossibility" principle. The modern historian is able to exclude spirits from his consideration except as figments of the imagination, metaphor in various forms. For his skepticism about sixteenth-century beliefs and records he has a reason not readily available to most of the people he writes of: confidence that he recognizes the physically impossible very accurately. How are we to evaluate the evidence on witchcraft? Cohn's answer: "Stories which have manifestly impossible features are not to be trusted in any particular, as evidence of what physically happened."[7] This proscription seems to be basic to the method of historical criticism that most modern writers apply tacitly or explicitly in weighing evidence about the work of witches and magicians. Obviously as a rule of thumb it is well received in the twentieth century. Obviously, too, it is as arbitrary as the earlier assumption that with help from hell witches could do the deeds attributed to them.

Not all historians who doubt the help from hell agree with Cohn that its manifest impossibility renders untrue in every sense all testimony to it. "For persons in a state of hopelessness," says Keith Thomas, "attachment to the Devil symbolized their alienation from a society to which they had little cause to be grateful. In this sense the idea of devil-worship was not total fantasy. It had what has been called 'subjective reality.' "[8] One could, then, in a sense truly give himself to Satan and, presumably, believe in the whole scheme of such apostasy, including cult and conspiracy. But Cohn sticks to the touchstone of the physically possible: "The same people who accepted that a cult of Satan existed, also accepted that Satan miraculously materialized at the celebration of his cult. . . . The two beliefs were practically inseparable; and if the one seems to lack evidential value, so should the other."[9] Perhaps to rule out evidence of the devil cult on such grounds is a little like saying that if there is no Allah there are no Mohammedans; but the fact remains that we probably lack a sounder test for basic evidence on the witch conspiracy.

The force of confessions. What of the large body of witches' confessions that convinced many nineteenth-century writers of the reality of the cult? Cohn concedes that "intelligent, educated, and devout men" accepted most confessions. But even the voluntary ones were likely to be given by people who "believed things about themselves which fitted in perfectly with the tales about heretical sects" that devoured babies and otherwise misbehaved. On these few "spontaneous" confessions Inquisitors piled confirming ones wrung out by torture and leading questions.[10]

Still, the genuine belief of many confessing witches and the acquiescence of the majority of learned and able men who studied them surely deserve some respect. We have to "admit their fundamental 'subjective reality,' " says H. R. Trevor-Roper. Jean Bodin, "undisputed intellectual master of the later sixteenth century," found himself confronted by a moving, unforced confession to *maleficia*, to attendance at Sabbats, and to sex relations with the devil. "Bodin admits that such a story seemed strange and almost incredible at second-hand. But he had heard it himself; he was a man of the world; and he was personally convinced of its spontaneity. Who are we to doubt his conviction?"[11] Whether or not any widespread conspiracy of devils or witches existed objectively, it certainly existed in the public imagination as generally and threateningly as, say, the dangers of nuclear power generation do in ours. Even in England, as we can see from the depositions and confessions that C. L'Estrange Ewen published in 1929 and 1933, the devil and devil worship were prominent in court proceedings. English law usually took some cognizance of demonic presence and purpose in witchcraft.[12] *Maleficium* **paramount.** Nevertheless, according to the British historian Alan Macfarlane, the people who brought accusations of witchcraft in Scot's England were "mostly uninterested in the compact with the Devil . . . or any presumed attack on Christianity,"[13] and Ewen's material says nothing of witch assemblies before 1600. Thomas, too, thinks that the "victim" cared far less about any religious deviation on the witch's part than about the injuries he suspected her of authoring.[14] *Maleficium* was the heart of the ordinary Englishman's complaint against witches. Certainly, as we have said, English prosecutors did not push charges of pact and Sabbat nearly as hard as Continental ones did, nor could the English interrogators use torture to help them tutor the accused in making their confessions orthodox. The witchcraft that Scot investigated in Kent and Essex was much tamer than that of which he read with horror and disgust in Bodin's work.

As Macfarlane insists through several chapters, what moved most English accusers of witches was an "atmosphere of fear and hostility" produced by problems of economics, health, and such "social phenomena" as name-calling, fights, threats, thefts, and accidents. These frictions often originated in churlish refusal of traditional door-to-door charity to the resentful poor.[15] Indeed, Thomas holds that bewitchment and suspicion of bewitchment characteristically arose from this breakdown of the medieval communal understanding that the better-off persons of a village were to sustain their impoverished neighbors with handouts.[16] A householder who stingily and callously turned away an old woman asking help and watched her leave muttering was likely, if he then fell into sickness or other troubles, to recall his own offense and the witch's displeasure. "A person who felt he had been bewitched would . . . identify the suspect by asking himself who might be likely to bear him a grudge. . . . The witch was not thought to be acting out of vindictiveness; she was avenging a definite injury. . . . The important point is that, paradoxically, it tended to be the witch who was morally in the right and the victim who was in the wrong."[17]

Guilt and prosecutions. This guiltiness of the "victim" enhanced, Macfarlane indicates, his tendency to charge witches before the court. "People needed to find some rationalization as to why they felt uneasy when they refused traditional obligations and Christian precepts which stressed that charity to those slightly worse off than oneself was a cardinal virtue. To find that the shunned neighbour, instead of righteously invoking the power of God through a widow's curse, was an evil old witch was a considerable relief."[18] The victim thus found his conscience cleared to prosecute.

When we read of witch cases now with such accounts of their origins as Thomas and Macfarlane give, we incline to sympathize with the alienated old woman, no matter what curses she may have mouthed. We may feel that her reaction outside the law was more defensible than its provocation, which was within the law. And that kind of sympathy was surprisingly alive in the sixteenth century. But not, naturally, among those who credited the effectiveness of witch curses. As Thomas makes fairly plain, the victim was in his own mind genuinely a victim, however uncharitably he might have turned the witch from his door.

For the *maleficium* that we casually discount was very real and frightening to its object and to his family and acquaintances. When a Protestant of Scot's time feared himself to be under the spell of witchcraft he might quite reasonably decide that it was a life-and-death matter. Although Ewen says that he never found an entry in coroners' rolls and inquisitions that ascribed death to witchcraft, his own abstracts of indictments show a decided majority in which the charge against the witch was causing illness, and in many it was causing death. The victim might, then, strongly incline to call in the law to make the situation as serious for the witch as she may have made it for him. He had hardly any other remedy. The "Catholic Church," Thomas says, "had provided an elaborate repertoire of ritual precautions designed to ward off evil spirits and malevolent magic. . . . A man who fell victim to witchcraft did not need to take his case to the courts since there was a variety of alternative procedures available. Indeed, a good Christian who used holy water, the sign of the cross, and the aid of the priest ought not to be so afflicted at all." But Protestant preachers "denied that such aids could have any effect. They reaffirmed the power of evil, but left believers disarmed before the old enemy." The readiest help against witches, then, might seem to be in "counter-magic." But the preachers called it as corrosive to the soul as any other resort to demons. So only "legal prosecution" was left.[19] It could, of course, lead "inexorably to the final remedy—the execution of the witch, as the only certain way by which the *maleficium* of the sorceror could assuredly and legitimately be brought to an end."[20] A Protestant who shrank from prosecution because of a Christian resolve to bear adversity patiently with fear of the Lord, could feel himself helplessly lost in suffering and death, his own and that of his loved ones. The pressure of this situation, Thomas thinks, may explain to some degree the rise in the number of prosecutions in England after the Reformation.[21]

Justification for prosecution. When a victim resorted to prosecution it was not necessarily from a self-excusing rationalization. The new national Poor Laws allowed local authorities to forbid casual alms-giving. The householder could, therefore, be in a real quandary when a dangerous-looking person solicited gifts. "I am loathe to displease my neighbor Alldridge, for I can never displease him, but I have one mischance or another amongst my cattle," says a troubled farmer in 1580.[22] And "as often as not, the link between the misfortune incurred and the obligation neglected was furnished by the frank expression of malignity on the part of the suspected witch." Some such persons, however imaginary their witch powers, must have been by temperament quite as grasping and vicious as the worst of those who slighted them. Thomas seems to say that no Iagos (or devil's servants?) were among the witches; we can "rule out the possibility of motiveless malignity" since the witch "was always believed to bear some previous grudge." But there is no denying a frequent Iagoesque (or devilish?) disproportion between the reason for the grudge and the supposed counterblow.[23] Enough to make a villager nervous.

Two other authorities, Jeffrey Burton Russell and Rossell Hope Robbins, do not think that the villager's fear of *maleficia* initiated witch cases in a way to account for the statistical rise in the number of them. They hold that responsibility for the craze lay more with "the intellectuals . . . than with the ignora-muses," since the printing press enabled the dissemination of

the "works of the witch theorists in a quantity hitherto un-
dreamed of" and so "added enormously to the growth of the
. . . craze.''[24] But a writer on Bodin, Richard Baxter, says that
this notion that the theorists "foisted their own fevered imaginations on to innocent old women" (not to mention nervous villagers in general) is a doubtful one, for "it would seem that the
pressure for witchcraft persecution arose from below." Thomas
thinks that in England, anyway, "most trials can be shown to
have originated at a local level, to have reflected local animosities
rather than to have been initiated from above." The trouble
was not, he says, "between the very rich and the very poor,
but between fairly poor and very poor.''[25]

The utility of witchcraft. Thomas finds, then, a self-con-
tradictory kind of social utility in the witch beliefs of the English
countryside. First, they "helped to uphold the traditional obligations of charity and neighborliness at a time when other social
and economic forces were conspiring to weaken them. The fear
of retaliation by witchcraft was a powerful deterrent against
breaking the traditional moral code." An "old woman's reputation for witchcraft might be her last line of defence, ensuring
that she was decently treated by her fellow-villagers." And so
"witch-beliefs may be fairly described as 'conservative social
forces.' " But, second, "they could have a more radical function," for some believers "stressed that it was dangerous to
give anything to a suspected witch, and advised she be ostracized
by the community." So "witch beliefs . . . upheld the conven-
tion of charity and neighbourliness, but once these conventions
had broken down they justified the breach and made it possible
for the uncharitable to divert attention from their own guilt
by focussing attention on that of the witch. Meanwhile, she
would be deterred from knocking at any more unfriendly doors
for fear of swelling the ranks of her accusers." Thomas concludes
that "in England, as in Africa, the belief in witches could thus
help to dissolve 'relations which have become redundant.' ''[26]

If the witch belief thus simultaneously sustained village charity
and helped to phase it out, would anyone at the time have
praised either effect as Thomas seems to do? What the witch
did for charity, she evidently did as a by-product of extortion,
and the associated phasing-out service was simply the developed
resistance to her extortion. The meaning that it imparted by

experience to those involved was that witches played the extor-
tionist's part but lacked the power that extortionists need. And
this is what contemporary reformers of witch belief urged. In
their terms either firm resistance weakened the witch or she
was bluffing the whole time. Evidently these conclusions inter-
twine with those of Thomas. But Scot would never have spoken
of witchcraft in terms of its social utility, and if the idea had
been presented to him he might well have retorted that no
such service as Thomas points to could justify the practice; and
much less could any superstitious submission to blackmail by
witches.

Scot and Modern Opinion

On the first page of his study of witchcraft in England, Macfarlane quotes an anthropologist's statement that "no social phe-
nomenon can be adequately studied merely in the language
and categories of thought in which the people among whom
it is found represent it to themselves." Macfarlane adds that
this is "especially true in the study of the history of English
witchcraft beliefs."[27] And he may well be right as far as the
supernatural representations usual in the sixteenth century are
concerned. The work of Summers is an instance of how misleading such study can be. An important facet of history, nevertheless, are the views of those who live it. To misrepresent those
views by entirely abandoning their terms and the focus of their
attention may befit anthropology, but surely not history.

Thomas's conclusion on witchcraft's side effects is, like many
conclusions of those who study sixteenth-century witchcraft now,
necessarily externalized, generalized, and reductive. It is far dis-
tant from personal acquaintance with witches or experience with
their craft or with their prosecution. It is thus almost as different
from Scot's conclusions and as unavailable to men of his time
as the "psycho-historical speculations" are in which Cohn wonders whether the infanticide, cannibalism, and sexual orgies that
orthodoxy attributed to witches are really just the fantasies of
Europe's repressed desires, outrages imagined as a "ritual inver-
sion of Christianity" and fruit of a widespread "unconscious
resentment against Christianity as too strict a religion."[28] Such
explanations were unguessed at in Scot's time in anything like

Cohn's terms. Nevertheless, Scot put together and meditated upon (in his own terms and from his own point of view) not a few of these historians' opinions. They have in his work an immediacy that 400 years of distance largely robs them of. The *Discovery* sounds more like an extraordinarily able journalistic "study in depth" than like history recovered from randomly surviving documents and turned into the speculations that modern historians build.

The grounds of Scot's skepticism. Scot had little or no means of knowing whether in France and Germany or even in England witches formed an organized cult with regular and heavily attended Sabbats. But he could know, or at least feel confident, that nobody flew anywhere on goats or broomsticks. He could not know whether orgies went on, with cannibalism and infanticide, at witch gatherings. But he could assert with as much aplomb as Cohn himself that whatever backsides might there be kissed, none belonged to a genuine devil. For Scot grounded his testing of the evidence as firmly as Cohn does on the assumption that any contamination of testimony by impossibilities made it useless. And like Cohn, Scot felt sure that he knew the impossible when he saw it in witchcraft. Like Cohn, too, he passed from confidence about impossibilities to nearly equal confidence about improbabilities.

Scot presents in a passage of the *Discourse* Cohn's stand that, if we reject as impossible the materialization of Satan at cult meetings, we have to reject also the "practically inseparable" belief in the meetings and in the cult itself. "Some of these crimes [of *maleficium*] . . . are so absurd, supernaturall, and impossible, that they are derided by almost all men, and as false, fond, and fabulous reports condemned. . . . If part be untrue, why may not the residue be thought false? For all these things are laid to their charge at one instant. . . . If one part of their accusation be false, the other part deserveth no credit" (27).

But then, Scot shrugs later in the book, "the more unpossible a thing is, the more we stand in feare thereof; and the less likelie to be true, the more we believe it." Otherwise "these divinors, astrologers, conjurors, and couseners would die for hunger" (171). The difference is that what is academic exercise for Cohn is social experience for Scot.

In one of his dedicatory epistles Scot begins his case against impossible witch feats with the much-quoted statement of his skepticism: "My question is not (as manie fondlie suppose) whether there be witches or naie: but whether they can doo such miraculous works as are imputed to them." Can a man breakfast in Rochester and dine at Durham? Or "can your enimie maime you when the Ocean sea is betwixt you?" May "a carnall bodie become invisible?" And, leaving the impossible for the unlikely: "Is it likelie that the lives of all princes, magistrates, & subjects, should depend upon the will . . . of a poore mallicious doting old foole; and that power exempted from the wise, the rich, the learned, and the godlie, &c?" Then passing quickly back to the impossible: "Is it possible for man or woman to do anie of those miracles expressed in my booke, & so constantlie reported by great clarks? If you saie, no; then am I satisfied. If you saie that God, absolutelie or by meanes can accomplish all those, and manie more, I go with you. But witches may well saie they can do these things, howbeit they cannot shew how they do them" (xvii).

Nevertheless, Scot says later, witchmongers are so foolish that "it will not suffice to disuade" one of them "from his credulitie, that he seeth the sequele and event to fall out manie times contrarie to their assertion." Instead of acknowledging the impossible, he just turns to other witches "of greater fame," or he will "thinke he came an houre too late; rather than that he went a mile too far" (9). Also, Scot says in a tone appropriate to the modern scientist who scouts the notion of "spiritualism," the fact that witches cannot repeat their asserted marvels should tell against their credibility. "If witches could doo . . . miraculous things . . . they might doe them againe and againe, at anie time or place, or at anie man's desire: for the divell is as strong at one time as at another, as busie by daie as by night, and readie enough to doo all mischiefe, and careth not whom he abuses" (10).

Why doubt the witch's personal power? The formal reason is that to

everie action is required the facultie and abilitie of the agent or doer; the aptnes of the patient or subject; and a convenient and possible application. Now the witches are mortall, and their power dependeth

upon the analogie and consonance of their minds and bodies; but
with their minds they can but will and understand; and with their
bodies they can doo no more, but as the bounds and ends of terrene
sense will suffer: and therefore their power extendeth not to doo
such miracles, as surmounteth their owne sense, and the understanding
of others which are wiser then they. . . . We see that ignorant and
impotent women, or witches, are the causes of incantations and
charmes; wherein we shall perceive there is none effect, if we will
credit our owne experience and sense unabused, the rules of philosophie, and the word of God. For alas! What an unapt instrument is a
toothless, old impotent and unweldie woman to flie in the aier? Truelie,
the divell little needs such instruments to bring his purposes to pass.
(10)

Scot then ends with a sentiment reminiscent of Montaigne's
urbane reminder that to kill people by law we should have
"sharp and luminous evidence," not just confident "conjectures." It is very strange, he says, that we will imagine that
"to be possible to be done by a witch which to nature and
sense is impossible; speciallie when our neighbor's life dependeth upon our credulitie therein" (10–11).

   The law and the impossible. Nothing, he picks up again,
is possible in law that is impossible in nature. A judge does
not credit a confession to an impossible deed, as, for instance,
one that contradicts an ironclad alibi. Judge and jury will deliver
no sentence against a man who says that he killed someone in
Berwick at a time when they themselves saw him in London.
If witches say that "it is doone through the divels help, who
can work miracles; whie doo not theeves bring their business
to passe miraculouslie, with whom the divell is as conversant
as with the other?" Mischief imputed to witches happens where
no witches are and continues after witches are hanged. Why
"attribute such effect to that cause, which being taken away,
happeneth neverthelesse?" Witches sometimes "confesse voluntarilie that which no man would ghesse, nor yet beleeve, except
he were as mad as they; so as they bring death wilfullie upon
themselves" (38). Occasionally they confess what is possible,
as that they have killed by poison, and Scot stands "not to defend
their cause. Howbeit, I would wish that even in that case there
be not too rash credit given, nor too hastie proceedings used,"

for sometimes what they claim is such a thing as killing a child in the womb by giving the mother an apple, "when nothing was added thereunto, which naturallie could be noisome or hurtfull" (39).

Scot and Cohn. A difference is noteworthy between Scot's application of the principle of impossibility and Cohn's. Although both shrug off testimony that Satan was physically in evidence at Sabbats, pact signings, or anywhere else, Scot acknowledged the real existence of devils and their activity against men; Cohn does not find even their existence worth arguing. Whereas Cohn is free thus to dismiss supernature, Scot was face to face not only with witchcraft in daily life but with dozens of seriously meant and successfully communicated opinions on witches and devils as testified to beyond dispute in most men's eyes. In a Bible-believing age Scot was a Bible-believing man, though he interpreted much of scripture in his own way. Cohn, in a much less believing age, seems to feel that he would lose face if he ever noticed seriously the biblical testimony, much less accepted any of it.

The difference, nevertheless, between Scot's views and modern ones such as Cohn's is not so great as some critics of Scot's have suggested. Both Scot and Cohn consider the agitation of a witch's victim to be irrational and any peril to him self-induced. Scot says that only the credulous suffer from enchantments (399). The witch, on the other hand, faces thoroughly objective prison, trial, and hanging. The sympathy of both Scot and Cohn is nearly all for the witch; neither of them has imaginative rapport with the witch's victim. They seek to bring home to their readers not the horrors of demonism but those of a persecution founded largely upon fantasies of scholars and Inquisitors. Scot had no inkling of Cohn's historiographic disqualification of much of the documentary evidence that nineteenth-century historians had depended on for confirming demonistic organization, principles, and practices. But Scot could apply common sense. How ridiculous of Bodin to use fiction like Apuleius's *Golden Ass* as testimony to transmogrification and how foolish to think that Satan instructed witches to enlarge his kingdom and at the same time had them murder "so manie infants" whom they might later have recruited (59).

Distinction of witchcraft from magic. Unlike Cohn,
Scot proposed no essential gap between witchcraft and magic.
"We generalie condemne the whole art, without distinction,
as a part of witchcraft, having learned to hate it . . ." (236).
(Scot here speaks of that "art" given to "wicked, vaine, and
impious curiositie, as unto . . . numbers, figures, . . . and
words." He exempts "natural magic" from this censure.)
Learned "conjurors" (Weyer's black magicians) are not paltry
like witches; they "pass the degree of witches . . . and deale
with no inferiour causes," but bring angels from heaven and
devils from hell. They "raise up what bodies they list, though
they were dead. . . . They go not to worke with a baggage
tode, or cat as witches doo" (313). But for all their pretentious-
ness, they are identifiable with witches, for both are either self-
deceived about their powers or are cozeners. Anyone persuaded
that they can achieve the wonders they claim "may soone be
brought to beleeve that the moone is made of greene cheese"
(32). For among magicians was "yet never seene any rich man,
or at least that gained anything that waie; or anie unlearned
man that became learned by that meanes: or any happie man,
that could with the helpe of this art either deliver himself, or
his freends from adversitie, or adde unto his estate any point
of felicitie: yet these men . . . must exceed all others if such
things could be by them accomplished, according as it is presupposed" (329–30).

The *Discovery* nowhere makes any such contention as Cohn's
that devil pact and worship were integrated into a witchcraft
fantasy by a faulty fifteenth-century scholastic confusion of
witches with ceremonial magicians. But Scot's identification of
magic with witchcraft does present the hypothesis of fantasy
as strongly as does Cohn's discrimination of them. Scot was as
firm as Cohn in holding magic and witchcraft alike to be empty
of all content but what went with fraud or delusion. The distinction that Cohn makes—that witches submit to devils but magicians rule them—Scot notices as put forward by demonologists:
"witches make a league with the divell, & so doo not conjurors."
Bodin and others thought that the "league," the explicit pact,
made the witch more culpable than the magician (374). But
Scot holds the contrary, for the magus is blasphemous in his

informed effort to deal with hell by misuse of the names of God (175, 363) and scandalous in his elaborate effort to deceive the public. Scot's principal point is always that witches and magicians are one in the futility of their operations (395). Their common foolish or wicked pretense identifies them for him and brings magic along with demonology, astrology, and the occult in general into his book on witchcraft.

Scot's neglect of "high" magic. Scot notices briefly the two more respected kinds of magic—the theurgical and the Cabalistic—only to lump them with all other spirit conjuring as impious and as necessarily fraudulent. Agrippa, he says, having "searched to the bottome of this Cabalist art, saith that it is nothing but superstition and follie. Otherwise you maie be sure Christ would not have hidden it from his church." Cabalists "brag that they are able . . . to know the unspeakable mysteries of God." But theirs are "nothing but allegorical games . . . to delude and cousen the simple and ignorant" (160). As for theurgy, "wherein they worke by good angels," its "ceremonies are altogether papisticall and superstitious" (392), and as Agrippa says, "the more divine these arts seeme to the ignorant, the more damnable they be. But their false assertions, their presumptions to worke miracles . . . their popish ceremonies . . . their secret dealing . . . their bargaining with fooles, their cousening of the simple, their scope and drift for monie doth bewraie all their art to be counterfet cousenage" (393).

Scot on confessions. Scot faces as squarely as any writer of our time the fact that dozens of untortured witches confessed their actions willingly. He agrees with Cohn that they "believed things about themselves that fitted in perfectly with the tales about heretical sects."[29] (228–29)

One sort of such as are said to be witches, are women which be commonly old, lame, bleare-eied, pale, fowle, and full of wrinkles; poore, sullen, superstitious, and papists; or such as knowe no religion: in whose drousie minds the divell hath goten a fine seat; so as, what mischiefe, mischance, calamitie, or slaughter is brought to passe, they are easilie persuaded the same is done by themselves; imprinting in their minds an earnest and constant imagination hereof. They are leane and deformed, shewing melancholie in their faces, to the horror of all that see them. They are doting, scolds, mad, divelish; and not much differing from they that are thought to be possessed with spirits. (5)

Scot concluded, as Trevor-Roper does from Bodin's testimony to his conversion, that witches could be extremely convincing. They are "so firme and steadfast in their opinions, as whosoever shall onelie have respect to the constancie of their words uttered, would easilie beleeve they were true indeed" (5). Scot does not say as Trevor-Roper does that such conviction is a kind of truth. But he seems to be excusing the witch on grounds of her general deficiency for human society.

Scot on witchcraft's evil. Scot speaks so much and so scornfully of the attribution of various evils to witches as almost to leave the impression that they had no mind to do evil and that evils sensibly associable with them never appeared. He means, of course, only that those that did appear had other causes than the supernatural. He seems of Thomas's and Macfarlane's opinion that *maleficium* was the common charge in English witch prosecutions and that formal accusations originated usually in village tensions, especially the disagreements between beggars and those enough better off to be begged from. Scot does not assemble such an array of case histories as Ewen and Macfarlane do. Usually his method is homely description.

These miserable wretches are so odious unto all their neighbours, and so feared, as few dare to offend them, or denie them anie thing they aske: whereby they take upon them; yea, and sometimes thinke that they can doo such things as are beyond the ability of human nature. These go from house to house, and from doore to doore for a pot of milke, yest, drinke, pottage, or some such releefe; without the which they could hardlie live: neither obtaining for their service and paines, nor by their art, nor yet at the divels hands (with whome they are said to make a perfect and visible bargaine) either beautie, monie, promotion . . . or any other benefit whatsoever.
It falleth out sometimes that neither their necessities, nor their expectation is answered or served . . . but rather their lewdnesse is by their neighbors reproved . . . the witch waxeth odious . . . to her neighbours and they againe are despised and despited of hir; so as sometimes she curseth one, and some times another. . . . Thus in process of time they have all displeased her, and she hath wished

evill lucke unto them all. . . . Doubtlesse . . . some of hir neighbours
die, or fall sicke; or some of their children are visited with diseases
that vex them strangelie. . . . Which by ignorant parents are supposed
to be the vengeance of witches.

    The witch . . . expecting hir neighbours mischances, and seeing
things sometimes come to passe according to hir wishes, cursses, and
incantations . . . being called before a Justice . . . is driven to see
hir imprecations and desires, and hir neighbours harmes and losses
to concurre . . . and so confesses that she (as a godess) hath brought
such things to passe. (5, 6)

    The reasons of witches. Scot's merely parenthetical no-
tice above that witches are "said to make a perfect and visible
bargaine" with the devil parallels the modern historians' contention that the pact had only a secondary place in the scheme of
English witchcraft. Scot's account of village tensions over witchcraft turns almost entirely on the witch's rejection by her neighbors and their fear of her consequent malicious attack on them.
This does not seem to mean, though, that like Thomas, Scot
held the "witch . . . morally in the right and the victim . . .
in the wrong." For all Scot's sympathy with abused old women,
the *Discovery* does paint them as frightening and the householder
as in fact terribly troubled, however at fault in his treatment
of them and misled about their powers.

    The lack of religious comfort for Protestants, then, that
Macfarlane and Thomas make much of is implicit in Scot's work,
for his attacks on Catholic comforts are as unrelenting as those
of any Calvinist preacher. He ironically suggests as a substitute
for prayers to saints that the witch-afflicted turn to cunning
women, and he names some for their selection (*Discourse,* 443).
Actually, of course, he offers only a hardy skepticism—which
itself precludes prosecution of witches and what comfort the
victim might get from it.

    Scot says nothing suggestive of Thomas's view that the decline
of Catholic practices in England may have contributed to a rise
in the frequency of prosecution. Doubtless Scot had no statistics
on that. But his attacks on Romanist shields against witchcraft
are all linked to a concurrent pressing of the case for skepticism.
A person inexplicably hurt in body or goods might, after reading
Scot, be less inclined to blame witches for his troubles if the

doubts Scot raises about the justice of prosecution take any hold of him. Better try a doctor or a banker to mend his fortunes than a magistrate, and for the rest to endure affliction as Scot advises. Protestant doubts of Catholic remedies for witchery could extend, Scot seems to hope, to the witchery itself—and perhaps it often did.

Whether Scot supposed, as Russell and Robbins now do, that the literate classes infected the lower ones with an elaborated superstition that strengthened the tendency to prosecute or, as Thomas and others do, that most trials naturally originated with the common people is hard to say. Scot certainly talks often as though the focus of the trouble were in the villages, but he also talks a great deal about the provoking and, he seems to think, influential fancies of the witchmongers. Scot certainly gives no notice to the idea that either one had "social utility," as Thomas argues. The only usefulness he could connect with witchcraft would be in the abandonment of all belief in it and fear of it. The people had ceased to believe, he says, in the ridiculous fable of Robin Goodfellow, "and in time to come, a witch will be as much derided and contemned, and as plainlie perceived, as the illusion and knaverie of Robin" (105). Witches' practical confessions, he adds—that is, confessions to cozenage—sensible judges can elicit without the "extremitie of torture" that the Inquisition uses to get the ones it wants. The quiet and effective work of some English magistrates Scot regards as self-evidently progressive.

Views foreign to Scot.   Cohn's bold speculation that the advertised horrors of witch practices existed chiefly in the sick and subconsciously rebellious imaginations of the prosecutors and a few of those to whom they fed leading questions would have been foreign to both Scot and his foes. Both sides felt that some men somewhere would enact any evil that they could imagine and find a way to achieve. The witchmongers thought that with hell's help witches actualized it all; Scot denied the help and on grounds of logical and practical difficulties jeered at as much as he could of the remainder. He concedes, though, that "some of these crimes may not onlie be in the power and will of a witch, but may be accomplished by natural meanes. . . . Manie a knave and whore dooth commonlie put in execution those lewd actions. . . ." But can witches go in their hundreds to the Sabbat? We have no testimony to it except from witches themselves—obviously unreliable witnesses in view of their difficult position before their interrogators (19, 35). If a child of a witch dies or is missing, the unshakable presumption is that she killed it for the Sabbat feast.

Witchmongers concede, Scot notices, that some confessions are from persons melancholy or mad. But he does not suppose the orthodox opinions to be fruit of a psychiatric affliction endemic among those who build on the answers that witches give. Those opinions are either merely benighted acceptance of devils' part in witchcraft or they are venal. Catholic clergy and others, Scot avers, push witch prosecutions for the profit in them (12, 17). His account of the persecutions is a thoroughly practical-minded exercise.

No assumption of depth psychology, then, and few of religious doctrine prevent Scot from seeing the events of the witchcraft craze by the shrewd measure of ordinary experience. His sturdy empiricism helps him to come often into harmony with modern or semimodern views and to hold firmly to them at some cost to himself. A coherent stand for justice and mercy to sixteenth-century witches modern writers on witchcraft can make without risk, but Scot made it when what he contended for and demanded seemed to most of his contemporaries nearly indefensible. Scot's effort to defend his unorthodox opinion compelled him to deal at length with problems not troubling to us. For he also, of course, belonged to his own time, however much he may have foreshadowed ours.

Chapter Four

Scot in His Time

To say that although he was in some ways a forerunner of modern thought on witchcraft Scot was also by an obvious necessity a man of his own time does not mean that he followed consistently either prevailing popular opinion about witches or the rationalized ones of the learned. Usually he contested most of both and did it, as far as he could, on their own polemical footing. Not that he would play the demonological game or that of folk superstition, but that in denying on principle the phenomena characteristic of them he would examine them individually and often in detail and at length. He did not, like Cohn, simply wave them away. To defeat the witchmongers, he felt, he must rehearse and expose their contentions and must substitute convincingly his own account of the evidence they cited and the witnesses they brought.

Scot retained, of course, some of the prejudices of his time and place, as shown in his inveterate condemnation of Catholic practices and his declared conviction that women were lesser vessels. And of course he was ignorant and credulous about nature in a way that his time and place imposed. He acknowledged, for instance, though rather hesitantly, the power of the remora, a six-inch fish, to retard progress through the water of the grandest sailing vessel (237). His conception of what is physically impossible is certainly not abreast of the findings of our sciences. This limitation does not often seriously damage his case against the witchmongers; it does sometimes make it seem a little bizarre to us.

Scot on the Bible

The matter that perhaps more than any other differentiates Scot from our contemporary writers on witchcraft is, as we have seen, the amount of space and thought he gave to arguing scriptural evidence. Scot, like most of his contemporaries, felt bound to accommodate his opinions to God's word. If, in his zeal, he occasionally accommodated the word to his opinions that does not necessarily distinguish him from some other exegetes of much greater repute.

The limits of the possible. Below God, to whom all things are possible, the borders of the physically possible to creatures were in Scot's time darkly uncertain except as scripture seemed to shed light on them. The miracles of God, such as the Transfiguration of Christ, few Christians professed to doubt, and the prayerful feats of men whom God empowered were equally credited. With God's help Aaron did transform his rod into a real snake. In the opinion of many the story verified also the answering transformation by Pharaoh's magicians, though interpretation of their ungodly performance was, of course, not favorable. Most exegetes reasoned that the Egyptian serpents—evidently not in a class with the one that God provided for Aaron—must have been the work of demons and therefore illusory.

Did this hell-assisted prodigy certify a persisting power in later magicians to do equally extraordinary deeds? Christian thinkers were likely to respect the biblical analogy in such deeds, but with reservations. Thus Aquinas rejected a priori the possibility that postbiblical magicians could make good on the extravagant menaces with which they tried to intimidate demons. Magicians threaten, he says, "certain impossible things, as for instance that unless the [demon] who is called upon gives help, he who invokes him will shatter the heavens or displace the stars." Such a threat speaks ill for the magician because it is lying, and for the demon because the lying attracts him.[1] Aquinas's opinion depends for acceptance on an assumption of spontaneous incredulity ready in all sensible men. But the saint expected no such incredulity about devils' power to turn men into seeming wolves or to transport witches bodily through the air, an ability demonstrated by Satan's carrying Christ from the wilderness to the temple's pinnacle.

Although we now dismiss lycanthropy and witch's flight about as spontaneously as we do the displacing of stars, we have to recognize that, considering what knowledge St. Thomas and his readers had of the facts, what testimony to werewolves and

witch's flight they faced, he did indeed show these wonders
to be conceptually quite acceptable. We cannot expect that he
would write much of marvels, especially those in the Bible,
with the perspective of Ernest Renan, who took the New Testament account of demons to be simply a contemporary way of
speaking about phenomena that from his superior information
he could name quite differently.

Application of the "impossibility" principle. If Scot
had applied the impossibility principle uncompromisingly
enough to match Renan he would have had to explain away
not only the serpents of the Egyptian magicians but also that
of Aaron. That rejection he showed no inclination for, lacking
as he did Renan's nineteenth-century grasp of physical facts.
He could, though, sometimes be nearly of a nineteenth-century
turn of mind about the scripture that witchmongers cited. He
mentions repeatedly the accommodation of scriptural expression
to the rudeness of a particular era or to the weak comprehension
of mankind. Thus of the heaven-sent "lying spirit" in the mouths
of Ahab's prophets (I Kings 18–23) Scot says, "This storie is
here set forth in this wise, to beare with our capacities, and
speciallie with the capacitie of that age, that could not otherwise
conceive of spiritual things, than by corporal demonstration."
He cites Calvin (as he frequently does on such escapes from
the literal text) that "Where sathan or the divell is named in
the singular number, thereby is meant that power of wickednesse
that standeth against the kingdome of justice. And where manie
divels are named . . . we are thereby taught, that we must
fight with an infinite multitude of enimies" (432). In the same
manner speaking on how Satan "entered into" the serpent in
Eden: the devil's entering is "rather metaphoricallie . . . spoken, than literallie . . . the divell is resembled to an odious
creature, who as he creepeth upon us to annoie our bodies;
so doth the divell creepe into the conscience of Eve."

Scot takes pains to say, though, that he abhors "that lewd
interpretation of the familie of love, and such other heretikes,
as would reduce the whole Bible into allegories." He "will
not sticke to saie, that [spirits] are living creatures, ordeined
to serve the Lord in their vocation" (452–53). This did not
mean, Scot often insists, that they could do real marvels for
enchanters. As Calvin put it, the Egyptian magicians "were but

jugglers." Their snakes, Scot adds, were just tricks, whereas "God (of nothing, with his word) hath created all things . . . and dooth at his will, beyond the power . . . of man, accomplish whatsoever he list . . . as here he did by Moses in the presence of Pharao." To "affirme that Jannes and Jambres . . . by . . . all the divels in hell, could doo indeed as Moses did by the power of the Holie-ghost, is woorse than infidelitie" (259).

The impossibility principle applied to the Bible or to anything else in Scot's day or in ours will have variable and sometimes consensual results. The most any writer can do with it is to be reasonable and consistent in his application and hope that those who read him will agree spontaneously with his judgments. And so Scot wrote. He tried always to cut short the admission of what was possible to witch or devil, and he left unlimited what was divinely done. Prudently he did not argue a method of deciding what was possible and what was not, but just moved from case to case, attacking contradiction where he could find it in his foes' arguments and for the rest just trying to scorch credulity with his contempt and irony.

Scot's exegesis. Scot did name some exegetical principles. The chief of them he sets out briefly in one of his dedicatory Epistles: "For as nature without discipline dooth naturally incline to vanities, and as it were sucke up errors: so doth the word, or rather the letter of scripture, without understanding not only make us devoure errors, but yeeldeth us up to death & destruction" (xviii). This passage is Scot's notice that he will not always be reading the Bible literally.

Before getting down to heavy work on the most used and debated passages, Scot snipes provocatively from the shelter of the Bible at articles of witchmongers' belief that conveniently ignore some texts. "I have read in scriptures, that God maketh the blustering tempests . . . and that they bloe according to his will. But let me see any [witches] of them all rebuke and still the sea in time of tempest, as Christ did; or raise the stormie wind, as God did with his word; and I will beleeve in them" (1). Indeed, he shrugs a little later, "If all be true that is alledged of their dooings, why should we beleeve in Christ, bicause of his miracles, when a witch dooth as great wonders as ever he did?" (27).

Scot's opponents no doubt thought such sallies frivolous, and he may well have agreed, though adding that he but answered them on their own level. Dreadfully in earnest, they were often nugatory. Bodin and *Malleus Maleficarum,* Scot notices, seriously endorse as a test to know a witch her complete inability to weep. The *Malleus* warns, Scot says, that "she must be well looked unto, otherwise she will put spittle upon hir cheeks, and seeme to weepe." But alas that "teares should be thought sufficient to excuse or condemne in so great a cause, and weightie a triall! I am sure that the woorst sort of the children of Israel wept bitterlie: yea, if there were anie witches at all in Israel they wept. For it is written that all the children of Israel wept" (22). Scot, we see, was not above a literal interpretation that pointed to the witchmongers' folly. In discussing charms and amulets he notices that some people write out scraps of the Bible and wear them around their necks. If, he says, "the bare letter, can doo anie thing towards your ease or comfort . . . or that it were wholesome for your bodie or soule to weare them about your necke: . . . then I would wish you to weare the whole Bible, which must needs be more effectual than anie one parcell thereof" (233).

Biblical nomenclature. In his Epistle to the Readers Scot confronts them with some facts about the Bible and witchcraft that should give them pause. "Until you have perused my booke, ponder this in your mind, to wit, that *Sagae, Thessalae, Striges, Lamiae* (which words and no other being in use do properlie signifie our witches) are not once found written in the old testament; and that Christ himselfe in his gospell never mentioned the name of a witch . . . neither he, nor Moses ever spake anie one word of the witches bargaine with the divell, their hagging, their riding in the aire, their transferring of corne or grasse from one feeld to another, their hurting of children or cattell with words or charmes, their bewitching of butter, cheese, ale &c: nor yet their transubstantiation" (xxi). The reader who has perused and pondered as invited to do might well decide that biblical silence on so much of witchcraft largely relieved him of concern about it. To deny convincingly the presence in scripture of any word for *witch* as Englishmen used that term much reduced the standing of witchcraft as sin; the Old Testament command, "Thou shalt not suffer a witch to live," lost some of its contemporary application. To remove

all biblical warrant for such major articles of witchcraft's sophisti-
cation as pact, flight to the Sabbat, and transformation of men
into beasts weakened the notion of demonolatry and a conspiracy
of hell. And to point out the absence from God's word of familiar
maleficia of the English countryside might dim them in high
theory, however untouched it left the villager's anxiety.

Biblical analogues. In claiming that neither Christ nor
Moses said a word about pact, witch flight, or transformation
Scot was on fairly firm ground, though as we have seen, the
Bible did provide analogues, often feeble ones, to some items
of witches' belief. Does Isaiah speak of pact when he mentions
certain "scornful men" who say that they have "a covenant
with death, and with hell are we at agreement" (Isaiah 28:15)?
And St. Paul calls the sorcerer Elymas a "child of the devil"
(Acts 13:10). These passages were too brief and tangential for
witchmongers writing on pact to make much use of them. Scot
can safely ask, "How chanceth it that we heare not of this bargaine in the scriptures?" (37).

On flight and transformation the Bible equipped the witchmongers rather more strongly. Still, Scot is willing and ready
to take them on. He heads a chapter: "Of transformation, ridiculous examples brought by the adversaries for the confirmation
of their foolish doctrine." Some of the ridiculous examples Scot
finds in Bodin, who, he says, asserts that the devil "dooth most
properlie and commonlie transforme himself into a gote, confirming that opinion by the 33, and 34. of *Esaie* where there
is no one tittle sounding to anie such purpose." In a hot marginal
note Scot adds: "J. Bodin abuseth scripture to proove a lie"
(71).

Bodin relies, Scot says, on poets and popes, and "finallie,
he confirmeth all these toies by the storie of Nabuchadnez-zar."
Because that sinful Babylonian monarch "continued seven yeres
in the shape of a beast, therefore may witches remaine so long
in the forme of a beast; having in meane time, the shape, haire,
voice, strength, agilitie, swiftnes, food and excrements of beasts,
and yet reserve the minds and soule of women or men." Witches
turn themselves into wolves because "they usuallie eate children
as woolves eate cattell," and they turn other persons "into asses
. . . for that such have beene desirous to understand the secrets
of witches." Why witches sometimes turn into cats Bodin "al-

ledgeth no reason, and . . . to help him . . . I saie that witches are curst queanes, and manie times scratch one another or their neighbours by the faces" (71–73).

"These examples," Scot fears, ". . . might put us in doubt, that everie asse, woolfe, or cat that we see, were a man, a woman or a child." Bodin himself concedes that "none can create anything but God" and that the devil "cannot alter his forme. And lo, this is his distinction . . . the essential forme (to wit, reason) is not changed but the shape or figure. . . . Howbeit, I thinke it is an easier matter, to turne *Bodins* reason into the reason of an asse, than his bodie into the shape of a sheepe: which he saith is an easie matter; bicause *Lots* wife was turned into a stone by the divell." Just as though, Scot sighs, "God . . . who also destroied the citie of Sodome at that instant, had not also turned her into a salt stone" (74).

Scot asks troublesome questions about beast-men. Suppose one died in the beast's shape; what would he look like when he rose on Judgment Day? And a "man's bodie must be fed with bread. . . . Bodins asseheaded man must either eat haie, or nothing" (79). Finally, then, Scot gets back to Nebuchadnezzer, who did eat hay, and upon whose story witchmongers triumph "as though *Circe* had transformed him with hir sorceries into an oxe. . . . I answer that he was neither in bodie nor shape transformed at all . . . as appeareth both by the plaine wordes of the text, and also by the opinions of the best interpreters." Scot does not mention that the king grazed, and says, without explaining, that he was "rather turned into the shape of a fowle than of a beast. . . . Howbeit, this . . . was neither of divels nor witches dooing; but a miracle wrought by God, whom alone I acknowledge to be able to bring to passe such workes at his pleasure" (81).

Satan's transportation of Christ. Scot passes on then to the matter of transportation of witches, for which almost the sole biblical analogue is that of Christ by Satan from the wilderness—"Which if he had done in manner and forme as they suppose, it followeth not therefore that witches could doo the like; nor yet that the divell would doo it for them at their pleasure. . . . I hope they will not saie, that Christ had made anie ointments, or entred into anie league with the divell . . . or that the divell could have maisteries over his bodie, whose soule he could never laie hold upon." If the deed was "wrought by the speciall providence of God," it is no good for the witch-monger's case, and anyway the whole thing was "in a vision, and not in veritie of action." Calvin agrees that it was a vision. That the devil showed Christ "all the kingdoms of the world, and the glorie of the same, and that to be doone (as it is said in *Luke*) in the twinkling of an eie, dooth more agree with a vision than with a reall action." Calvin's statement, Scot declares, "differs not one syllable nor five words from that which I had written herein, before I looked for his opinion in the matter" (82–83).

Bible's words translated "witch." As for the Old Testament words translated *witch*, none conveys the sense put upon *witch* in Scot's day. The *Praestigiatores Pharaonis* were "but couseners and jugglers . . . making false things appear as true: which nevertheles our witches cannot doe." *Mecasapha* signifies poisoner. *Kasam, Onen, Ob,* and *Idoni* all pertain to "sundrie kinds of divination." A fifth word, *Habar,* Moses uses of "magicians, or rather such as would be reported cunning therein" and that "mumble certeine words, wherein is thought to be great efficacie" (87).

If this last seems not to fit well the case that Scot is trying to make, still he goes on undismayed. Because translators use *witch* for all these words, the "common people, who have never hitherto beene instructed in the understanding" of them, believe easily. So, says Scot, he will show "the opinion of our age; speciallie of *Johannes Wierus,*" who himself "singularlie learned in the toongs, yet . . . sent for the judgment of *Andreas Massius* the most famous *Hebrician* in the world" (87). Scot then begins a seven-book treatment of the words translated *witch*. The discussion gives him great scope for alleging misdirection and fraud. But it does not fully justify his earlier contention that the Bible has no word reasonably translated *witch* unless we part the fundamental idea of witch from that of magician or sorceror. And neither Scot nor Cohn has managed that parting conceptually, however social or educational accident may distinguish witch from magician experientially.

Scot's problems in biblical analogies. In his list of features of witchcraft missing from the Bible Scot does not mention three important items of demonology: demonic possession, necromancy, and the incubus. Of these, the most evident in scripture was certainly possession. It was prominent also in the attention of Englishmen about the time that Scot published and into the next century. It connected closely with witchcraft because the possessed might name persons in the community as having commissioned the possessing devil. Necromancy, the raising of the dead, usually to inquire of them about the future, was explicit in the enormously debated episode of the Witch of Endor. It touched the doctrine of personal resurrection. Did the witch raise Samuel as Christ did Lazarus (127)? The tale of coition of incubus and succubus with human beings was important in the theory of witchcraft as a symbol of the witch's vile submission to hell, especially at the Sabbat. But biblical support for it was so slight and so debatable that Scot might well have included it among those items that Christ and Moses did not mention.

The sole intimation in the Bible that spirits can cohabit with women is in Genesis 6: "the sons of God saw the daughters of men that they were fair: and they took them wives of all which they chose." And: "the sons of God came in unto the daughters of men, and they bare children to them." Scot says that Hyperius "hoovering about the interpretation of Genesis 6, from whence the opinion of *Incubus* and *Succubus* is extorted . . . seemeth to mainteine upon heare-saie, that absurd opinion; and yet in the end is driven to conclude . . . there can be no firm reason or proofe brought out of scripture" (69). Scot did not trouble to say that St. Augustine had established the opinion that the Sons of God in Genesis were not angels but the progeny of Seth.

The Witch of Endor. With the necromantic feat of the Witch of Endor, though, Scot had no such easy time. The immense discussion of it was not only by those most concerned with witch theory but by the general run of commentators. For skeptics the tale that I Samuel 28:8–20 told was forbiddingly straightforward and seemingly literal. Saul visited a woman who had a familiar spirit for divination. He demanded of her, "Bring me him up whom I shall name unto thee. . . . Bring me up Samuel." When the woman saw Samuel come up, she cried out, suddenly knowing the king. She described the man she saw, and "Saul knew that it was Samuel. . . . And Samuel said to Saul, Why has thou disquieted me, to bring me up?" He then told Saul his doom, to be fulfilled during the coming day.

Interpreters with a Platonist bent were very likely to suppose that the witch did indeed raise the shade of Samuel or some other physical remnant of him. Catholics held that by divine interposition she truly raised the soul of Samuel, but Protestants such as Ludvig Lavater (very influential in England a few years before Scot published) insisted that the apparition was a devil usurping Samuel's form. Scot, going as usual his own difficult way, wrote the whole affair off as fraud. He treated it in his seventh book, given to elucidating the Hebrew word *Ob,* which he said was improperly translated *Magus* but properly *Pythonicus* or *Ventriloquus.* To illustrate what such folk were like, Scot related his story of the fraudulent "Pythonesse of Westwell" in Kent, who told many things in a devilish voice but was at last exposed. Scot then took up "Bodins stuffe" about the Pythonist of Endor (101–6). He got so wrapped up in the "stuffe" and in the tale of a "counterfeit Dutchman" that he postponed Saul and Samuel and rambled on through five more chapters, mainly about "Apollo, who was called Pytho," before he finally got back to the necromancy at Endor.

Did the "Pythonissa" raise up Samuel from the dead, "inforce his verie resurrection"? Well, says Scot, "He that . . . looketh into it advisedlie, shall see that *Samuel* was not raised from the dead; but that it was an illusion or cousenage practised by the witch." Scot conceded that some exegetes of good standing held that "God interposed himselfe . . . to bring *Samuell* when the witch would have raised her divell. Which is a probable interpretation." But Peter Martyr speaks "more to the purpose": the thing must "have beene done by Gods good will, or perforce of art magicke: it could not be doone by his good will bicause he forbad it; nor by art, because witches have no power over the godlie." Besides, "*Samuel* was directlie forbidden to answer *Saule* before he died: and therefore it was not likelie that God would appoint him, when he was dead, to do it" (112).

Having thus set aside the argument that Samuel came "up" by divine interposition, Scot reinforced Peter Martyr's dismissive opinion that "art magicke" could not have raised a blessed soul. Scot scorned the question, of course: "For what quiet rest could the soules of the elect enjoy or possesse in Abrahams bosome, if they were to be plucked from thence at a witches call and commandment?" That way "should the divell have power in heaven" (113). True, "Necromancers affirme, that the spirit of anie man may be called up . . . before one yeare be past after their departure from the bodie." Agrippa (whom Scot respected for his recantation on magic) says in *Occult Philosophy* that it may be done by "certaine natural forces and bonds." But Augustine and others who deny "the raising of Samuell," conclude that "the divell was fetcht up in his likenesse: from whose opinion (with reverence) I hope I may dissent" (114).

A second biblical source for the raising is Ecclesiasticus 46:19–20, which has it that Samuel "before his long slepe" made an imposing statement about his own probity and then "after his slepe also he told of the kings death." This passage had troubled Augustine, and Scot began his five-chapter exposition and defense of his own opinion that the whole affair was cozenage by using Ecclesiasticus against Augustine's conclusion. Scot asks, "If the divell appeared and not *Samuell;* whie is it said in Eccle. that he slept? for the divell neither sleepeth nor dieth."[2] Scot's answer to his rather confusing question is that the truth of the matter was in the fact that the whole affair was a description of "the deceived opinion and imagination" of Saul. That the Witch fooled him is the obvious and sensible thing to conclude. "For it is ridiculous (as Pomponacius saith) to leave manifest things and such as by natural reason may be prooved, to seeke unknowne things, which by no likelihood can be conceived, nor tried by anie rule of reason." The devil was not raised, nor was Samuel either, and the whole thing may well have been deception by the "cunning of the woman" (114).

Applying Pomponazzi's principle, Scot entered then on one of his thorough, commonsense reductions of the marvelous to the ordinary, of the supernatural to mundane contrivance. The Witch, he snorts, was sister to the fake Pythoness of Westwell, and Saul was brother to a man cheated by a juggling sorcerer whom Scot knew (116). Plainly, Saul lived near Endor, for he came and went in a night and had time for a meal there. And besides, he was the tallest man in Israel, so the Witch recognized him immediately, though she pretended not to in order to lend force to her performance. Saul saw nothing of what she claimed to see. She told him what he expected to hear—of an old man in a mantle. Since Samuel was famous, she would know about his mantle. It, sniffs Scot, was of course "consumed and rotten" in the grave, but "belike he had a new mantel made him in heaven: and yet they saie Tailors are skantie there, for their consciences are so large here" (118).

The Witch probably had a confederate, Scot decided, to play Samuel's part. He seems to forget here his opinion that Samuel was not visible to Saul. Or perhaps Scot just neglected to state his agreement with opinion expressed by the translators of the Geneva Bible and by others[3] that as the séance progressed Saul did see and hear. Scot indicated, though, that the woman spoke in a rumbling, ventriloquistic voice for Samuel, so perhaps the confederate did not speak. The Witch had guessed, Scot says, that Saul's "heart failed"; to suit his mood she decided on a gloomy prediction. That what she gave was not heaven's prediction or even hell's appears in its inaccuracies. One of Saul's sons survived the battle; after death "wicked Saul was not with good Samuel!" and the battle did not take place the next day as she said it would (120).

Scot concluded his argument by again speaking respectfully of the "opinions of some learned men, that Samuel was indeed raised, not by the witch's art of power, but by the special miracle of God." Scot still rejects this reading, apparently because he hesitated to call a biblical marvel divine unless the text did so explicitly, and because it would have brought him to the Catholic position. Of it he just notes that "the papists saie, that it cannot be a divell, because Jehovah is thrise or five times named," and such naming "Satan cannot abide." Anyway, Scot decided, on this bit of scripture "arguments are daielie devised, to proove and mainteine the miraculous actions of witchcraft, and the raising of the dead by conjurations. And yet if it were true, that *Samuel* himselfe were raised, or the divell in his likenesse . . . it maketh rather to the disproofe than to the proofe of our witches," for they cannot duplicate the feat (121). With this soundly arbitrary circle in reasoning Scot finally dropped the hot potato that the story of the Witch of Endor handed him. He would, he said, stake his life on witches' inability to raise the dead.

Demonic possessions. An even hotter potato than necromancy was demonic possession and exorcism. Scot dealt at length with not a single one of all the explicit and apparently literal episodes of them from the New Testament. In his *Discourse on Devils* he touched briefly on the Old Testament case of Saul's affliction by an evil spirit that God sent (I Samuel 16) and on Satan's entering the serpent in Genesis. The latter, however, belongs chiefly to his treatment of whether devils had power to acquire a body. Scot denied it and explained the "entering" as a fiction of those who do not understand that *serpent* in Genesis is just metaphor for *Satan* (451). As for Saul's evil spirit, Scot sneered that *Malleus Maleficarum* takes it to mean that when the music of David's harping drove it from Saul, "the departure of the divell was by means of the signe of the crosse imprinted in David's veines." That reading just showed, Scot felt, how absurd men could be when they spoke of such matters without warrant of the Bible (431).[4]

Of the New Testament possessions Scot notes in the *Discourse* only that:

As touching those that are said in the Gospell to be possessed of spirits, it seemeth in manie places that it is indifferent or all one, to saie; He is possessed with a divell; or He is lunatike or phrenetike: which disease in these daies is said to proceed of melancholie. . . . But who saith in these times with the woman of Canaan; My daughter is vexed with a divell, except it be presupposed that she meant hir daughter was troubled with some disease? Indeed, we saie, and saie truelie, to the wicked, The divell is in him: but we meane not thereby, that a real divell is gotten into his guts. . . . There was brought unto Christ one possessed of a divell, which was both blind and dumbe, and he healed him: so as, he . . . both spake and sawe. But it was the man, not the divell, that was healed, and made to speake and see. Whereby (I saie) it is gathered, that such as were diseased, as well as they that were lunatike, were said sometimes to be possessed of divels. (430)

In the *Discovery* Scot has only a sentence or so on Christ's exorcisms. "As for the casting out of divels (which was another kind of miracle usual with Christ), witches and conjurors are said to be as good thereat as ever he was." But it cannot be true, for Christ said, "If sathan cast out sathan, he is divided, &c. and his kingdome shall not endure, &c" (142).

The biblical accounts of possession were a trouble to Scot because they seem an almost undeniable assertion of spirits' physical action in the world without such divine empowerment as Aaron had to transform his rod. Scot had no choice but to interpret possession as metaphor for disease. But how the metaphor should have entered, with permission, into the herd of swine he does not undertake to explain.

". . . not suffre a witch." Scot's greatest problem with scripture was, of course, the text that most sustained persecution of witches, the laconic command in Exodus 22:18, "Thou shalt not suffre a witch to live." It stood inconspicuous among ninety-nine other "temporall and civile ordinances," as the Geneva translation has it. Against the usual and obvious interpretation Scot made a single mighty effort.

The key Hebrew word, he said, is *Chasaph,* "Latined *Veneficium,* and is in English, poisoning, or witchcraft; if you will have it so." The Greek of the Septuagint means, "You shall not suffer anie poisoners, or (as it is translated) witches to live." Josephus, a very learned man, "interpreteth in this wise: Let none of the children of Israel have any poison that is deadlie, or prepared to anie hurtful use." A person caught with such "stuffe" shall himself take it. "The *Rabbins* expositions agree herewithal." The word *Chasaph* is in nine other books of the Old Testament, and all English translations give it as *witchcraft* (89).

Scot shared the reluctance of his contemporaries to challenge a divine command, and he shared also their contentiousness about what exactly some divine commands called for. On one as explicit as Exodus 22:18 seemed to most readers, Scot could have had fights aplenty if he had wanted them. But he will, he says, avoid prolixity and contention—vices that he rarely shies from—and "admit that *Veneficae* were such witches as with their poisons did much hurt among the children of Israell; and I will not denie that there remaine such untill this daie, bewitching men, and making them beleeve, that by vertue of words, and certaine ceremonies, they bring to passe such mischeefes, and intoxications as they indeed accomplish by poisons." This sort of deception is the abuse that the text reproves, "together with taking Gods name in vaine . . . especiallie by the name of witchcraft, even where no poisons are" (89). Scot suggests that Simon Magus lived by such false witchcraft and that his effort to buy the power of exorcism from Paul showed how

impotent a magician Simon was as well as what an evil one
(90). Then, in half a dozen chapters, more or less on the subject
of what kind of witch should not be suffered to live, Scot dealt
with the views of only two witchmongers, and then only briefly.
After an excursus on love potions, Scot rebuked Leonard Vair
for saying that "Christ and his apostles were *Venefici*" and Bodin
for faultily accusing Weyer of a mistranslation from the Greek
for *poisoner* (99). The points Scot tried to make against these
two are neither very clear nor very relevant to the controversy
on whether the text in Exodus speaks only of poisoners or also
of those who claim to have a witch's powers but do not have
them or of those who, as the orthodox interpretation went,
claimed such powers and did have them.

Scot's powers and problems.   In his resistance to the orthodox opinion on Exodus 22:18 Scot leaves the same impression he did when contesting texts on demonic possession; he
seems steadfast but troubled. He was steadfast in his early and
persisting contention that witches have no supernatural power
in themselves and that devils can give them none. He was troubled by the difficulty of making his stand credible in the face
of so flat-footed a biblical statement as the Exodus law seemed
to be. As always, he did his best, though hampered by his natural
honesty. Perhaps he did dilute that honesty a bit on this question
and on that of demonic possession by neglecting more than
usual the arguments of the other side. Like many a case-making
journalist of our own time, he was confident that he was right
but knew that his public was deeply mired in a contrary opinion,
which in justice and the common interest somebody should try
to revise. He seems to have felt a vocation for the job.

He had a keen sense of demonology's inventive departure
from credible and viable accounts of men's daily living and
an equally keen sense of bitter injustice done. He had considerable powers in polemics, and a scholarship reasonably sound.
He had also a solid if unspectacular piety in England's established
religion. These things show in his treatment of biblical interpretation as in all other matters of religious controversy. Scot saw
that for many of his countrymen the Bible was a fabric of "superstitions" that fueled foolish fears and angers. He saw, too, that
for many cool-minded and learned men it was a kind of cosmic
map, an elucidating authority for partisan rationalizations that

needed anchorage in revealed truth. He himself belonged to a class of practical persons, like Queen Elizabeth, to whom the Bible was primarily a respected document of ceremony and order, not wholly perspicuous but serviceable if searched with common sense. Scot naturally applied his common sense to all superstitious readings and to many ideological ones, though of course he acknowledged the authority of God's word for establishing a useful cosmic picture.

What Scot seems to have had no grasp of was the enthusiasms of one who read the Bible as a source of mystical devotions. To him the *Proposopeia* of Thomas Lodge (a Catholic convert) was, we may guess, nonsense and his *The Diuel Conjured* just demonological superstition. In his distaste for mysticism Scot was, perhaps, well beyond his time, which was shaping enthusiasts for such works as those of Sir Henry Vane and John Pordage and had already, besides Lodge's, those of Nicholas Breton, Robert Southwell, and others.[5] But in his distaste for Catholics and their often ingenuous elaboration of their devotional practices and reasoning, Scot was entirely of his time and place.

Scot's Attacks on Papistry

A twentieth-century editor of the *Discovery* says that Scot as "a child of his age" in which Protestants were "violently persecuting both Catholics and witches," tried to "identify the two" and it "involved him in much theological foolishness."[6] The editor had in mind, perhaps, such an extravagance as the chapter that Scot wrote "against the papists abominable and blasphemous sacrifice of the masse," a rite, he said, uncivil and cruel to Christ (153). But this and similar passages were not so much "foolishness" as they were routine Protestant persiflage. Similarly polemical, though not theological, is Scot's rudely stated opinion that passages in St. Augustine's writings that seem to subscribe to witchmonger views must "be foisted . . . by some fond papist" into the body of the saint's work (76). To us these slurs against Scot's fellow Christians seem unbecoming, certainly, and not really calculated to help quiet the craze against witches. But they were in the tone of Scot's times and probably pleased many readers.

Scot does not attempt "to identify" Catholics with village

witches so much as with the ceremonialists he usually calls
"sorcerors" or "conjurors." The effort goes on throughout his
work. Derision of Catholic rite and doctrine as superstitious
crops up in a few paragraphs of nearly every book and in a
majority of chapters. But the concentrated and systematic identification comes in book 15, "whereby the whole art of conjuration is deciphered." After twenty-one chapters of such
decipherment of secular magic, including "an inventorie . . .
of divels," a statement of how they "may be bound," "an experiment of the dead," and "how to enclose a spirit in a christal
stone," Scot gets to "a comparison betweene popish exorcists
and other conjurors." He professes to see no difference between
the magical conjurations and popish ones "but that the papists
doe it without shame openlie, the others doo it hugger mugger
secretlie." The papist "officers . . . are called exorcists or conjurors, and they look narrowlie to other couseners, as having
gotten the upper hand over them." In order that the world
may see the papists' cozenage and impiety "to be as great as
the others," Scot will, he says, cite one conjuration (he "might
cite a hundred") that is "knaverie and cousenage in the highest
degree." Its purpose is to detect the cause of "spirituall rumbling
in houses, churches, or chappels, and to conjure walking spirits"
(365).

   Flaws in Scot's case.   There is no denying that the prepara-
tory purgations for this operation as Scot gives them much resemble those he had picked for comparison from the *Lemegeton.*
The actual "conjuration," too, the prayer that addresses the
spirit, resembles those secular ones in Scot's earlier chapters.
The Catholic office is, however, conspicuously free of such gross
acquisitiveness as "I conjure thee spirit N. by God the Holie-
ghost, the which dooth sanctifie all faithful soules and spirits
. . . to declare the true waie, how we may come by these trea-
sures hidden . . . and how to have it in our custodie" (361).
Nor do "church magicians" summon devils to serve them in
lust, greed, and revenge as, by Scot's showing, the lay ones
do.

   Besides ignoring these differences, Scot gives no consideration
to the probability that the rites of magic were modeled largely
on those of the church; and if that had been called to his attention
he might have snorted that the debt could as well be the other

way. Whichever way it was, the resemblance of Catholic rites to magical ones was in Scot's eyes damning for both of them. If he had at hand, as he claimed, a hundred clerical conjurations to reinforce his point, he forebore any such procession of them as he had provided of the lay ones. Before showing any more at all he digresses into a long tale of a discreditable monkish effort to distress a bereaved husband for revenge or profit by means of a fake demonic voice that declared his wife's soul to be in hell. Then a long chapter relying on Aquinas and the *Malleus* describes the order of exorcism and derides seven papist reasons why exorcism sometimes does not rid the possessed of their devils.

Further examples of "clerical magic." A short chapter follows full of caustic comment on "gross absurdities," and finally three brief Catholic conjurations. First, "I conjure thee thou creature of [holy] water in the name of the father, of the sonne, and of the Holie-ghost, that thou drive awaie the divell . . . that he remain not in the darke corners of this church and altar." A second is to clear devils out of certain water that it may be safe for drinking; and the third is an "exorcism for incense." With these, Scot will, he says, "for brevitie let all passe" (375–76). He then sums up: "The rules and lawes of popish Exorcists and other conjurors are all one." Both papists and magicians undertake "to absteine from sinne, and to fast, as also otherwise to be cleane from all pollution, &c." Both use "divine service and praiers," the secular being "in the same papisticall forme, no whit swarving from theirs in faith and doctrine, nor yet in ungodlie and unreasonable kinds of petition" (377). Here, certainly, Scot either errs or lies, for the Catholic petitions are to drive out devils, not to bring them in, and for cleansing, not for help in sinning. Nor is it easy to see how Scot could have supposed that the Catholic office was one "in faith and doctrine" with magical ones that sought not only to intimidate finite spirits but to bind deity itself—unless, of course, we suppose, as Scot certainly did not, that all prayer is an effort to constrain.

Substance of Scot's charge. In his comparison of church rites with those of lay magic Scot was not charging either one with *maleficia* or diabolic compact, but both with credulity and superstition or fraud and larceny, and with blasphemy, deliberate or not. For he says elsewhere (bk. 12, chap. 4) that God has forbidden witchcraft "bicause of the abuse of the name of God and the cousenage . . . therein" (177). He concludes his comparison in chapter 30 of book 15 with the heading "That it is a shame for papists to beleeve other conjurors dooings, their owne being of so little force." Papists, who above all others insist on the force of witches' charms and of "conjurors cousenages, should perceive and judge conjurors dooings to be void of effect," for they see "their owne stuffe, as holie water, salt, candles, &c." and their consecrations all ineffectual. They adjure holy water to heal illness and candles not to consume, "yet neither soule nor the bodie anie thing recover, nor the candles last one minute longer" (379).

   Another attack. In book 12 Scot has another concentration of chapters against church magic, concerned this time with "inchantments, certaine wordes, verses or charmes" (174). He gives several pages of "Popish periapts, amulets and charmes" worn or recited to save from wounds, sickness, thievery, and "evils present, past, and to come, inward and outward." Then after a chapter on "how they make their holie water" and a couple on the opinion of a physician that charms may indeed help in psychosomatic cures, there are pages of folk charms, mixed occasionally with others, presumably more sophisticated, from Bodin, Paracelsus, Danaeus, and the like. Scot strongly implies that they should know better. These charms secure against "the biting of a scorpion," toothache, headache, locked doors, and a dozen other afflictions. Most of them do not seem at all handy, and a good many call for materials of dubious antecedents. Thus: "A charme to release a woman in travell, Throwe over the top of the house, where [she] lieth, a stone or any other thing that hath killed three living creatures; namelie, a man, a wild bore, and a she beare" (197).

   Scot means the whole display to impress the reader as ridiculously gullible and wicked. He ends the book by noting that neither the Apostles nor anyone else in the primitive church carried or recited charms, nor did Christ "use or command holie water, or crosses, &c.: to be used as terrors against the divell. . . . Let us then cast awaie these prophane and old wives fables." At the last day the "heathen philosophers" may well expose the "infidelitie and barbarous foolishness of our Christian or rather anti-Christian and prophane witchmongers." Aristotle and Socrates, Scot notes, affirmed the vanity of enchantments, Galen averred that disease was always natural, and Hippocrates that spells are cast by knaves and cozeners (233).

Scot's Protestantism. From time to time Scot gives notice to the fact that Catholic opinions resemble not only thaumaturgical ones but respected Protestant ones. In the *Discourse* he provides a considerable list of Protestant credulities matched to Catholic. "We are sure the hollie maide of *Kents* vision was a verie cousenage: but we can credit, imprint, and publish for true possession or historie, the knaverie used by a cousening varlot at *Maidstone* [a tale Scot had told in bk. 7, chap. 3] and many other such as that was" (446). He ends valiantly his comparative recital: "Whereby I gather, that if the protestant beleeve some few lies, the papists beleeve a great number. This I write, to shew the imperfection of man, how attentive our eares are to hearken to tales" (447).

Modern writers do not find it easy to praise Scot's virulent anti-Catholicism—except those who are themselves anti-Catholic, usually by way of being also anti-Christian and antireligious. These, if they like, may read Scot with assurance that he would have spoken as they do if he had thought that he could get away with it. To read Scot so requires only the extension to deity of the veiled unbelief in finite spirits that some historians suspect lurked in him.

But Scot's anti-Catholicism is that of a Protestant of his time and place, not that of an unbeliever or even a doubter. Certainly what he takes to be absurd presumption of ceremonial powers irritates him as a rationalist. But it also infuriates him as a Protestant. Though he may have in no way been a mystic or "enthusiast" of any sort, he was a believer in God as "maker of all things, judge of all men," and found his faith well enough articulated in the Anglican communion with, no doubt, a Calvinist shading. His religious sincerity will not make his harsh judgment of Catholicism more palatable to most modern thinkers who are themselves religious, but it does help to fix him as a man of his time.

Chapter Five

Scot's Peculiar Contentions

Just as his temperament excluded Scot from the raptures of biblically inspired enthusiasts so did it exclude him from the learnedly rationalized ones of those Renaissance humanists who wanted to mesh the Bible with Hermetic and Cabalistic mysticism. Although he knew something of ancient Neoplatonists through their translator, Marsilio Ficino, and of the legendary Hermes Trismegistus and was occasionally respectful of them, Scot showed no attachment to such ideas as that the universe emanated from God as a single organism responding in every part to every other. Nor did he care for the depending claim that men might rise back through the stages of divine emanation toward the originating wholeness of being. And less still did the deviations of mysticism into power magic attract him as its sponsors maneuvered among gods and daemons who answered to arcane symbols that secretly initiated men could display to them. Scot's tastes in learning were rather of the Reformation than the Renaissance. He did not yearn, like Pico della Mirandola, to improve Christianity and convert the Jews by the reinterpreted wisdom of the *Aesclepius* and the *Zohar.*

Ceremonial Magic

The clearest and firmest idea about magicians that Scot stressed in the *Discovery* was that since he knew some of them for frauds, the rest must be the same, though as yet unexposed. The Cabala of the higher mysticism, the "real" Cabala,[1] Scot scarcely noticed. The "fantastic" or "practical" Cabala, the conjuring one, and its equivalent in Hermeticism, he supposed to be plainly self-serving and, at best, vain. Although he tended to excuse witches as persons whom law and custom abused, he was wholly adverse to magicians, holding them to be impious scoundrels and impostors. Whether deluded or deluding, they acted, he thought, from desire for power and riches by means that were not only delusory but idolatrous and hubristic. And they got worldly returns enough from their vile work to need no help or sympathy.

Witches, Scot indicates, though fools about magic, are petty ones. For whatever their pretensions to power, they go from door to door for relief, but "conjurors are no small fooles." They have "gotten them offices in the church of *Rome,*" and they carry about "books intituled under the names of Adam, Abel, Tobie, & Enoch" and others that they say Abraham, Aaron, Solomon, or even "angels Riziel, Raziel, and Raphael" wrote. Magicians know the arts Almadell, Notoria, Bulaphiae, and Revelationis, which they claim came down from Moses (380–81). They invoke devils instead of angels because "(as Agrippa saith) Good angls (forsooth) doo hardlie appeare, and the other are readie at hand."[2] Agrippa, "who in his youth travelled into the bottome of all these magicall sciences, and was not onlie a great conjuror and practiser thereof, but also wrote cunninglie *De Occulta Philosophiae . . .* recanteth his opinions, and lamenteth his follies." In later life he disclosed "the impietie and vanities of magicians, and inchanters, which boast they can doo miracles: which action is now ceased (saith he) . . . affirming that this art teacheth nothing but vaine toies for a shew" (382).

Scot concedes that wise men such as Plato, Pythagoras, Empedocles, Democritus, and the magi who adored the infant Christ have traveled the world to learn the art of magic—but it was "naturall magicke." Solomon was the greatest traveler of them all for this purpose, as appears in Ecclesiastes and "the book of *Wisdome.*" These important personages meant to learn the magic that comes with knowledge of nature, and they meant to preach and teach it. But "without great heed be taken," Scot thinks, "a student shall soone be abused." Natural magicians may be "wise men," "philosophers," "priests," or "prophets"; but still magic has an infamous part to it, "given unto wicked, vaine, and impious curiositie, as unto moovings, numbers, figures, sounds, voices, tunes, lights, affections of the mind, and words" (235–36).[3]

Danger in magic. This warning that anything called magic could be dangerous to meddle with was, of course, an echo of dozens like it from all sorts of clerics and from many magicians. It had its place, especially in the work of Christian Hermeticists and Cabalists. Ficino spoke for a kind of magic but was intensely concerned to keep all question of spirit invocation out of it. His astrological "cantiones," he insisted, were not incantations to demons. Johann Reuchlin wanted an "operative magic" and found it particularly in the Cabala, which, he thought, cleared magic of diabolism since it worked only through good angels and other holy forces by means of the names of God. Pico held that to be safely on the side of heaven the magician must proceed always by means of the Cabala.[4] Both Pico and Ficino supposed, too, that the descriptions they gave of the universe brought such magic as they spoke for into a realm of nature, making it a discipline that they could study and use as part of creation's seamless totality beneath God. So in a sense their operations were natural. They had to admit, though, the existence of evil daemons and the danger that even natural magic would slide over into traffic with hell. They defended themselves nervously against the charge that their magic had so slipped.[5]

Agrippa followed in the track of Pico, Ficino, and Reuchlin in his desire for a holy magic of power, and he was less cautious about it than they were. His *Occult Philosophy* was "intended," says Frances Yates, "to be a very white magic" of mingled Hermetic and Cabalistic origins. "The function of Cabala as Agrippa saw it, was not only to provide the highest 'supercelestial' magic, but to guarantee the safety of the operator against demons at all levels." She adds, though, that "the genuine Hebrew Cabalist might be shocked by Agrippa's interpretation of Cabala as solely white magic." And in fact, notes another modern authority, Agrippa's magic was "overtly demonic, recklessly unorthodox."[6] Like many magicians of worse purpose, Agrippa spoke piously but showed some operations hard to fit into the Christian scheme of right conduct, much less of right worship. For Agrippa's magic as the *Occult Philosophy* describes it requires an operator with the "power to consecrate" attained by initiation and discipline and used in observances of invocation that include prayer and sacrifice to spirits. Except in miracles, Agrippa explains, no man rules spirits by the direct power of God. So the magician must win the help of finite "gods" with "holy rites comformable to the condition of every one." Whoever "invocates the gods and doth not confer on them their due honor, rightly distribute to them what belongs to them, shall neither enjoy their presence, nor any successful effect from them."[7] Obviously such invocation was a kind of worship that Protestant theologians did not allow while Catholic ones allowed it just barely to some heavenly angels. Further, Agrippa's text plainly indicates that through angels or divine names the magician might hope to command devils. This dubious operational theory, along with seriousness of purpose and confidence of results, makes the doctrine of magic in the *Occult Philosophy* one that Scot could countenance no more than Bodin could, although the two were far apart in their reasons and statements.

Scot needed the ostensible skepticism of Agrippa's *Vanity of the Arts and Sciences* and so was content to accept it as sincere and total recantation. He does not notice that some years after the appearance of the *Vanity* Agrippa revised the much-circulated manuscript of the *Occult Philosophy* and published it. Bodin, on the other hand, tarred Agrippa with the name of sorcerer by ignoring the *Vanity* and accepting as genuine a fourth book of *Occult Philosophy,* which Weyer, who should have known, stoutly insisted was spurious. And, indeed, however reckless and unorthodox the three-book *Occult Philosophy,* it was not a "grimoire," a handbook of demon-summoning by an operator greedy for action. The real Agrippa usually sounds like a man of elevated mind. The so-called *Fourth Book* is not at all in his vein. But neither Scot nor Bodin had any polemical reason for acknowledging either innocence or elevation in Agrippa's magic. Scot wanted to find all spirit magic blasphemy and insolent pretense to special powers; Bodin preferred to find apostasy and a fearful diabolical power. Each picked out what suited him.

Manuals of black magic. The *Fourth Book* is typical of works of black magic. The *magicien infame* that Weyer acknowledges to be for all practical purposes simply an educated witch— that is, a practicing devil worshiper—could find the *Fourth Book* bound in several sixteenth-century editions with the first three and with the even more explicit *Heptameron or Magical Elements* (falsely attributed to Peter of Abano), and with some fragments from Trithemius and others. The *Heptameron* is a detailed instruction manual for the raising of other-worldly beings who, to judge by their names and offices, are no spirits of health.

Besides the printed grimoires, and probably more used than they, were the manuscript ones, especially the Solomonic rituals. *The Key of Solomon* may originally have been in Hebrew, but it apparently circulated in western Europe during the sixteenth century chiefly in French. *The Lemegeton* or *Lesser Key,* Weyer knew as the *Liber Spirituum,* and from it he took the explicit material in his *Pseudo-Monarchia Daemonum* that Scot duplicated in his lists of devils and his examples of incantations. Weyer apparently had only the first book, called *Goetia,* which was entirely on black magic. Scot seems to have had access to other sources besides Weyer, probably a manuscript copy (see my chapter 2, note 17).

All of these books of magic, and perhaps others, Scot may have seen in whole or in part. They gave him ample room to denounce both imposture and blasphemy in magic. The *Fourth Book* speaks of writings in blood to attract an evil spirit and of lights, perfumes, unguents, and medicines that "do partly agree with the spirit . . . and partly are exhibited to the spirit for religious and superstitious worship."[8] The *Heptameron* conjures jointly the Archangel Michael, one of the three angels of God mentioned in scripture, and the demonic "king" Varcan. It uses names of God and barbarous cries: ". . . in the name of *Adonay, Eye, Eye, Eye . . . Eye, Abray. . . .* I conjure thee, *Michael,* Oh! great Angel . . . That thou labour for me, and fulfil all my petitions, according to my will and desire, in my cause and business."[9] In fear for his soul Bodin turned his gaze from such demonic raving, and he condemned Weyer for printing some of it, though the purpose of that printing was to expose the vile practices of ritual diabolism.[10] And with contempt and repulsion Scot reprinted the incantations: ". . . I require thee, O Lord Jesus Christ, that thou give me thy Vertue & power over all thine angels (which were thrown down from heaven to deceive mankind) to drawe them to me, to tie and bind them & and also to loose them . . . that they obeie me and my saiengs and feare me" (328).

Scot's case against magic. Scot's intention was to accent the gap between the imposing power source the operators appealed to and the pettiness, vanity, and impiety of their purposes as bound to the feeble breath of their means. Before he gets to his exhibitions from the *Lemegeton* Scot says repeatedly that the magician's means, especially his incantations, are worthless, must be worthless. Not "all the conjurors, Cabalists, papists . . . inchanters, witches, nor charmers in the world" by either "humane or yet diabolical cunning" can bring marvels to pass. "For by the sound of words nothing commeth, nothing goeth, otherwise than God in nature hath ordeined to be doone by ordinarie speech, or else by his special ordinance" (175). But the witchmongers thought otherwise. Bodin did insist, indeed, that "to say that the power of words achieves something is evidently a trick of devils which they are accustomed to use in order to trap the ignorant."[11] But he also insisted that devils came eagerly to the blaspheming sorcerer and did bad deeds for him. Marlowe used this ancient orthodox idea in *Dr. Faustus.*

After he has given us thirty-odd pages of devils' names, titles, and powers and the incantations to rule them, Scot says that he did it to show "the vanitie of necromancers, conjurors, and such as pretend to have reall conference and consultation with spirits and divels: wherein (I trust) you see what notorious blasphemie is committed, besides other blind superstitious ceremonies, a disordered heap, which are so far from building up the endeavours of these black art practitioners, that they doo altogether ruinate & overthrow them" (363). Conjurors are "more faultie than such as take upon them to be witches, as manifest offenders against the majestie of God . . . and violators of the lawes and quietnesse of this realme: although indeed they bring no such thing to passe as is . . . urged by credulous persons, couseners, liers, and witchmongers." Magicians are "alwaies learned, and rather abusers of others than they themselves by others abused" (363).

Fraudulent claims. What "truth or possibilitie is wrapped within these mysteries"? Magicians claim that they can work miracles, call devils and souls from hell, and "when they have gotten them shut them in a circle made with chalke . . . so stronglie beset . . . with crosses and names, that they cannot for their lives get out." These spirits the mages bind and loose and "make them that have been liers from the beginning, to tell the truth. . . . And the divels are forced to be obedient to them, and yet cannot be brought to obedience unto God their creator" (364).

Scot then gives us his chapters on church magic with, as we

have seen, some specimen "conjurations . . . out of the pontifi-
call and . . . the missal," before coming back for a final polishing
off of black magic. "J. Bodin confesseth, that he is afraid to
read such conjurations, as John Wierus reciteth; least (belike)
the divell would come up, and scratch him with his fowle long
nailes . . . I for my part have read a number of their conjurations, but never could see anie divels of theirs" (374). Perhaps,
Scot muses, the devils know that he will not do business with
them; but of course Bodin thought that whoever recited the
conjurations was in fact doing business.

Witchmongers say constantly, Scot notices, that witches should
be worse punished than conjurers because witches make pacts
whereas conjurors shield themselves with their devil-summoning
rites. But if ritual really brings devils why will they not come
when Scot uses it? "Oh absurd credulitie!" The "art" is so
contrary to God's word that if one is true the other must be
false (374).

Tests of magic. Scot's test of magic by reading from grimoires is one of the few recorded efforts in his time to apply
an empirical standard to the claims of believers. If learned men
"would make experience, or duly expend the cause, they might
soon be resolved" (374). Scot's challenge to them, says one
authority on him, was to "produce under controlled circumstances, even one verifiable instance of the operation of diabolic
magic."[12] Scot tells us of an experiment of Johann Baptista Porta.

Porta had got from an "old witch" (who may, Scot cautions,
have fooled him) the "receipt" for a flight-enabling ointment.
Another willing "witch" tried it out for him. Having smeared
herself, she "fell down through the force of those soporiferous
or sleepie ointments into a most sound and heavie sleep." Porta
and his staff could not arouse her. When she awoke she "impu-
dently" affirmed that "she had passed over both seas and moun-
tains" and insisted on many false reports in the face of their
earnest denial. Although Scot does not seem convinced of the
genuineness of the recipe, he does seem to think Porta's investigation a creditable one and the result an embarrassment for
the witchmongers, whom it "greatlie overthroweth" (148–49).

So Scot considers Porta and others whose concern is natural
magic to be on a right track in both method and purpose. God
has hidden mysteries in nature and man may penetrate them,

though "to sluggards, nigards, & dizzards," the secrets of nature are never opened, since to learn even its trivial secrets requires great pain and cost. But "doubtlesse a man may gather out of this art, that which . . . shall set foorth the glorie of God, and be manie waies beneficiall to the commonwealth." Investigators should publish their discoveries and skillfully apply them to mankind's use and service (237). Scot had no more patience with holy ignorance about nature than a modern scientist does. He was as eager as anyone to explore her mysteries.

Magic and science. Still, the language of his time bound him to think of such exploring in terms of magic. He noticed, as Ficino, Pico, and Reuchlin did, that natural magic was hard to set off conceptually from spirit magic if spirits were a part of nature, and he acknowledged that some of the penetrations of nature's mysteries were so ill-understood in their causes as to seem "miraculous . . . if it be true that *J. Bap. Neap.* and many other writers doo constantlie affirme" that the "feathers of an eagle consume all other feathers, if they be intermedled together." As for the "little fish being but half a foot long" that "staieth a mightie ship,"—well, says Scot, it is "affirmed by so manie and grave authors, that I dare not denie; speciallie, bicause I see as strange effects of nature otherwise: as the propertie of the loadstone . . ." (237–38).

Plainly the reductionism that Scot so boldly applied to the witch's marvels affirmed by many grave authors he did not always use, nor did he always depend on "experience," as he recommended witchmongers do. Why did he not bundle up some eagle feathers with dove feathers and see what happened? Simply, we may decide, because life is too short to investigate everything personally. Besides, William Gilbert himself, who did investigate the "loadstone," could not understand it better than Scot could. It seemed to Gilbert to act like a soul, "or as a fragment of the Soul of the Earth."[13] Scot labored as well as he could to make the difference between spirit magic and what we call "science" a usable one, to put science entirely in the realm of man under God and free of demonic forces acting in the physical world. It was an enterprise in which Robert Boyle succeeded sixty-odd years after Scot wrote.

When Henry More attacked some of Boyle's conclusions on hydrostatics with the claim that spirits were obviously active in the phenomena that Boyle had observed, Boyle replied that More was trying to accommodate the phenomena to his hypotheses, not testing the hypotheses against the facts. Given God's laws for nature, Boyle said, "the explication of what happens among inanimate bodies" is sufficiently made by "the motion, bigness, gravity, shape, and other Mechanical affections of the small parts of the liquores." He did not intend "to prove that no angel or other immaterial creature could interpose in these cases; for concerning such agents, all that I need say is, that in the cases proposed we have no need to recurr to them."[14] Scot could have no knowledge of such experimenting as Boyle's, but Boyle's principle would have appealed to him immensely.

Scot's Exclusion of Spirits

The chief means by which Scot tried to keep the idea of natural magic free of spirit magic was the same one he used to keep his idea of witchcraft free of it: he excluded spirits from magic by denying that they were at all physical or had any physical powers. If not original in this, he was yet distinctive. Sadducees and Socinians were said to deny the existence of spirits, and Pomponazzi denied it in order to justify his thesis that only celestial bodies transmitted God's power. But, of course, unlike these scorners, Scot accepted spirits as creatures given beyond denial in many passages of the Bible. They were created for a work peculiarly their own. Only he insisted that such work was all "spiritual," entirely a matter of tempting by the evil angels and of defending from temptation by the good. So men who called on spirits for apparition and for service to their greed and lust called in vain. This was a twist of demonology very nearly peculiar to Scot in the England of his time.

As Scot's account of magic in the *Discovery* and the *Discourse* is confined almost wholly to black magic, so his account of spirits deals principally with devils, since good angels appear little in the tales and theories of black magic. Scot ignored, too, as we have seen, most of the characteristic demonological questions on spirits' substance, classes, ranks, numbers, dwellings, and occult sympathies. He preferred just to deride the elaborate expositions of witchmongering experts on these things. He would gladly have done the same, we gather, for the physical powers of demons, for he was always reluctant to enter controversy on the ground of his foes' expertise. When he had to do so, he usually turned the struggle over to authorities convenient to his use. Chief among them on the work of spirits were Calvin and Peter Martyr of Vermigli. But, as usual among Scot's helpers, they did not always say just what would have helped him most.

On apparition. On the vital question of whether spirits appeared and acted in the temporal world, Scot wanted to deny both the assumed body that scholastics said a spirit could shape from an element and the rarefied one contractible into visibility that Platonists held native to finite spirits. Daemons, Scot notes in the *Discourse,* "doo varie" in substance; some think they are of air, others of fire, and "some of the starres and other celestial powers. But if they be celestial, then (as *Peter Martyr* saith) must they follow the motions of those elements of which their bodies consiste." They cannot be air, for of it no distinct members may be made. Scot then launches away from Peter: spirits' bodies cannot be of water, or they would moisten the place where they stand, nor of fire, or they would burn what touches them (433–34).

Catholic angelologists were contemptuous of such objections, but many Protestants, though strong for the temporal work of spirits, did want to hold that apparition was not within their ordinary power. Peter Martyr in the passage that Scot uses is extensive but at last vague on the whole matter. Air will not do for a body peculiar to a spirit; still, spirits do assume sensible bodies and have the power to act in them, as they show through magicians, and these assumed bodies are airy and need not have bodily organs. In another place in the same work Peter says that the "schoolmen be compelled to devise another shift." They say "that Angels, if they be compared with men, are spirits: but if with God, they have bodies, because they are destitute of the single and pure nature of God." This not very helpful distinction was a commonplace much older than scholasticism[15] and settles nothing about apparition. Peter seems finally willing for his readers to think as they like so long as they understand that the Bible and general experience confirm apparitions. On the whole he seems at last somewhat more against Scot than for him.

After citing Peter rather disingenuously, then, Scot went boldly on to declare apparition impossible for devils. Their essence and form, he averred, were so proper to them as to be unalterable by any finite power. "For we find not that a spirit can make a bodie, more than a bodie can make a spirit: the spirit of God excepted, which is omnipotant" (454). Scot never grappled fully with either scholastics or Platonists on this matter. Probably, though, his reticence did not hurt his case with many of his readers, since it suits the general Reformist trend (cf. 425). Calvin says more than once that he dares not affirm anything about angels but what scripture tells him of them.[16] Such angelological depreciation of angelology was quite evidently a step toward neglecting it. But neglect was not, of course, quite the same thing as Scot's explicit exclusion of spirits from physical nature.

Demonic venery. Early in the *Discovery* Scot notes that Bodin and half a dozen others he names "doo make a bawdie discourse . . . to prove by a foolish kind of philosophie, that evill spirits cannot onlie take earthlie forms and shapes of men; but also counterfit hearing, seeing, &c. . . . and devoure meats . . . reteine, digest, and avoid the same: and . . . use diverse kinds of activities, but especiallie excell in the . . . art of venerie." Truly, Scot concludes, these versatile assumed bodies seem far superior to the ones that God made in paradise, "so the divels workmanship should exceed the handie worke of God the father and creator of all things" (58). Such highly developed bodies could be visible or invisible at the devil's pleasure. Indeed, the *Malleus* has it that "manie times witches are seene in the fields and woods prostituting themselves . . . naked up to the navill, wagging and mooving their members in every part, according to the disposition of one being about that act of concupiscence, and yet nothing seene of the beholders upon hir: saving that after such convenient time as is required . . . a blacke vapor . . . hath been seene . . . to depart from hir" (60).

Scot then converts to merry tales some serious items from legend and the *Malleus* on devilish venery. Most he aims at papists, as in the case of a certain lady who took offense at an incubus's overtures and cried out. Rescuers found that devil under her bed in the likeness of "the holie bishop *Sylvanus*," who "was much defamed therebie" until a devil confessed at St. Jerome's tomb to having played the bishop's part. The *Malleus* testifies, Scot says, that incubi prefer blondes (62, 63).

Error about Lucifer. Scot did not hesitate to apply the same sort of ridicule to the revered legend of Lucifer's rebellion in heaven and ejection from it. The witchmongers "falselie conceive the commensement of divels out of the fourteenth of *Isaie,* where they suppose *Lucifer* is cited, as the name of an angell; who on a time being desirous to be checkmate with God himselfe, would needs (when God was gone a little aside) be sitting downe, or rather pirking up in God's owne principall and cathedrall chaire." For this insolence God threw Lucifer and "all his confederates" out of heaven. Some fell to the bottom of the earth, some but to the "middle region, and the taile of them having not yet passed through the higher region staied even then & there, when God said, Ho." But of course, Scot remarks, *Lucifer* signifies in Isaiah only the morning star, and stands for Nebuchadnezzer.[17] A little later Scot touches scornfully on the multitude of opinions about how Michael and his angels "overthrew *Lucifer,* and turned him and his fellowes out of the doores." But, he shrugs, the *"Sadducees* were as grosse" as the schoolmen, for "they said, that by angels was ment nothing else but the motion that God dooth inspire in men, or the tokens of his power" (423). In his quips against angelologists Scot does not let his reader forget that angels, both good and evil, are real creatures.

The nature of devils. What, then, are these real creatures like? Well, "they have their laws and limits prescribed, beyond the which they cannot passe one haires breadth," the devil having "none other powr, but that which God from the beginning hath appointed unto him . . . which is, that he being a spirit, may with Gods leave and ordinance viciat and corrupt the spirit and will of man: wherein he is very diligent" (80).

In the *Discourse* Scot paraphrases Augustine, who "saith . . . that sathan or the divell while we feed, allureth us with gluttonie: he thrusteth lust into our generation . . ." and so on through the list of the deadly sins. "When we wake, he mooveth us to evill works; when we sleep, to evill and filthie dreames; he provoketh the merrie to loosenesse, and the sad to despaire" (426). But there is not "any such corporal communication betweene the divell and a witch as witchmongers imagine" (86). Fraudulence marks most testimony to demons' ordinary speech with man, Scot thinks, and he gives examples of it. For instance, a devil through the mouth of his medium "answered men to all questions" until one was put in Latin, with which language the unlettered devil had no acquaintance (401).

"Mine own opinion and resolution of the nature of spirits and of the divell, with his properties" comes near the close of the *Discourse.* The opinion and resolution Scot sustains here is from Calvin and from his own kinsman M. Deering, whom he presents as authorities with good sense. Like them, he depended at last wholly upon scripture. Satan is a "creature made by God, and that for vengeance . . . and of himselfe naught, though emploied by God to necessarie and good purposes." Satan was evil from the beginning. When God at the creation saw that all that he had made was good, Satan was "not comprehended within those words of commendation," for he was a murderer from the beginning and the father of lies.[18] God did not make him in that first week, but "created him purposelie to destroie." His substance is such "as no man can by learning define," so that St. Paul in his modesty confessed a "holie ignorance of the state of angels: which name is also given to divels." They lie daily in wait to corrupt and ruin mankind, "being the verie tormentors appointed by God to afflict the wicked in this world with wicked temptations, and in the world to come with hell fier" (454).

Scot was, we may believe, expressing here a genuine and literal belief in the existence of devils and in inward tempting as their sole power upon men. He considered this view and resolution ample for the Christian faith; King James and many others would call it "error" if not heresy. But as demonology it was certainly bold and far more clear-cut than any opinions that Calvin or Peter Martyr or other pillars of Protestantism put on record about the powers of devils.

The Force of Excluding Spirits

If Scot was convincing in his contention that devils could have no temporal communication with witches, his position against the witchmongers became far stronger than Weyer's, which depended wholly on acknowledgment that the witch was too ignorant and too weak to agree responsibly with devils. She could not thus vitiate her baptism and load herself with the "irremisible" Sin Against the Holy Ghost. Scot used these arguments to the full (55 ff.) but from the solid base that the closest the witch came to meeting the witchmongers' description was when she deceived herself that she had seen a devil. Weyer's arguments and Scot's alike included the corruption of judges and Inquisitors, the extortion of confessions, and the delusions of both victims and prosecutors. But in discussing these devil-managed delusions, as he thought them, Weyer drifted helplessly, whereas Scot steered firmly to the conclusion that no problem existed. Devils could not in any ordinary way fool a man's senses. Men just fooled themselves. And as for temptation, Scot adds, I Corinthians 10 promises that none shall be tempted above his strength; most accused of witchery are so weak that their responsibility cannot be great. They are "unlearned, unwarned, and unprovided of counsell and freendship," void of judgment and discretion. And if by some strange chance the witchmongers should be right, we must think witches overawed by a devil "in shape so ugglie, as *Danaeus* and others said he is." Therefore, Scot concludes, "I see not, but we may shew compassion upon these poor soules; if they shew themselves sorrowfull for their misconceipts and wicked imaginations" (30).

The witch's pact. The "plaine bargaine" that the witch thinks herself to make with the devil and that many declare "so horrible and intollerable" requires of the witch "homage" and a grant of "both hir bodie and soule to be tormented in everlasting fire" (31). Now, one might suppose that "the divell sometimes . . . should meete with some that would not consent to his motions . . . and so should be bewraied. They also (except they be idiots) would spie him and forsake him for breach of covenants" (35–36). And anyway, "Mee thinketh their covenant made at baptisme with God . . . sanctified with the word, confirmed with his promises, and established with his sacraments, should be of more force" than the usually unwitnessed one that they can make with the devil. "For God deceiveth none, with whom he bargaineth; neither dooth he mocke or disappoint them, although he danse not among them" (37).

Then follows a chapter headed "What follie it were for witches

to enter into such desperate perill, and to endure such intollerable tortures for no gaine or commoditie, and how it comes to
passe that witches are overthrown by their confession." The
helpless old women are simply "daunted with authoritie, circum-
vented with guile, constrained by force, compelled by feare,
induced by error, and deceived by ignorance . . . and are so
brought to absurd confessions." Anyone who observes them
closely "shall perceive that melancholie . . . hath deprived or
rather depraved their judgments, and all their senses: I meane
not of coosening witches, but of poore melancholike women,
which are themselves deceived" (40).

Through all such Weyerian exposition of the witch's luckless-
ness, Scot threads mention of his own basic stand: all talk of
pact, no matter how voluntary the confession of it, is vain and
false, for what "bargaine can be made betwixt a carnall bodie
and a spirituall" (34)? Everyone "having the gift of reason may
plainlie perceive, insomuch as it is manifest unto us by the word
of God, that a spirit hath no flesh, bones, nor sinewes, whereof
hands, buttocks, claws, teeth and lips doo consist" (37). By
what "authoritie, proofe, or testimonie; and upon what ground
all this geere" of the pact stands the reader may see in the
Malleus Maleficarum, "to the shame of the reporters . . . and
to the reproch of the beleevers of such absurd lies." And "if
the league be untrue, as are the residue of their confessions,
the witchmongers arguments fall to the ground" (34).

   The Sabbat.   Along with the pact Scot attacks the kindred
fantasy of the Sabbat. At certain solemn and public assemblies
the witches not only see the devil "but confer and talke familiar-
lie with him." He exhorts them to fidelity and promises long
life and prosperity. He examines novices to see if they are "apt
and forward in renunciation of Christian faith, in despising anie
of the seven sacraments, in treading upon crosses, in spetting
at the time of elevation . . . then the divell giveth foorth
his hand and the novice joining hand in hand with him,
promiseth to observe and keepe all the divels command-
ments" (31).

The witchmongers would have us to understand also that
after witches have "delicatlie banketted with the divel . . . and
have eaten up a fat oxe and emptied a butt of malmsie . . .
nothing is missed of all this in the morning," for everything

is magically restored, including the bullock; his bones reassemble and he "riseth up . . . in his former state and condition." All the time that a witch is at the Sabbat a serviceable devil occupies her bed "in so perfect similitude as hir husband . . . neither by feeling, speech, nor countenance can discern hir from his wife. . . . Wherein their credulitie is incredible, who will have a verie bodie in the feined plaie, and a phantastical bodie in the bed: and yet (forsooth) at the name of Jesus, or at the signe of the crosse, all these bodilie witches (they saie) vanish awaie" (33).

Witches' powers. Scot was, of course, equally contemptuous of other special contacts of men with demons and of the wonders supposed to result. Anyone who acknowledges God as the only author of miracles will "denie that the elements are obedient to witches . . . that they might at their pleasure send raine, haile, tempests, thunder, lightening; when she, being but an old doting woman, casteth a flint stone over hir left shoulder . . . or hurleth a little sea sand up into the element" or uses any of several other nonsense gestures "affirmed by writers to be the meanes that witches use" (47). If witches could in fact do the things attributed to them "then might they also be impediments unto the course of all other natural things and ordinances appointed by God; as, to cause it to hold up, when it should raine; and to make midnight of high noone: and by those meanes (I saie) the divine power should become servile to the will of a witch, so as we could neither eat nor drinke but by their permission" (48). But, he says elsewhere, he is sure that if all the witches in England were hanged not a drop less rain would fall (2).

Witches have confessed that sometimes they kill a man "with a touch of their bare hand . . . when all his garments are betwixt their hand and his flesh." It cannot be true, of course, for "the working of miracles is ceased," no "reason can be yeelded for a thing so farre beyond all reason," and, anyway, a power thus virulent and working simply through the witch's veins would be bound to kill the witch herself (39). The *Malleus* and Bodin, Scot repeatedly asserts, tell many such lies about witches, including some about their charmed invulnerability. One stood in the fire and did not burn until a "charme written on a little scroll" was removed from "betweene hir skin and flesh." Another the executioner was unable to strangle, "doo what he could" (23).

Such outright foolishness prosecutors fostered in many ways, most prominently by use of torture: "upon the racke, when they have once begunne to lie, they will saie what the tormentor list" (24). Plain misunderstanding, too, plays a part. For instance, the incubus is really a "bodilie disease . . . of thicke vapor proceeding from the cruditie and rawnesse in the stomach: which ascending up into the head oppresseth the braine. . . . To turne and lie on the one side is present remedie" (68). Also a disease is the conviction some men have that they change into beasts. It proceeds "partlie from melanchoie, where manie suppose themselves to be woolves. . . . J. Wierus declareth verie learnedlie the cause, the circumstance, and the cure" (81).

The Law on Witches

Scot turns from the fancies of diabolical phenomena to the facts of legal process. "Cardanus writeth, that the cause of . . . credulitie consisteth in three points; . . . in the imagination of the melancholike, in the constancie of them that are corrupt therewith, and in the deceipt of the judges; who . . . both accuse and condemne them, having for their labor the spoile of their goods." Scot shrugs pityingly. "There is no waie in the world for these poore women to escape the inquisitors . . . but to gild their hands with monie. . . . For they have authoritie to exchange the punishment of the bodie with the punishment of the purse" (27).

English law did not allow the torture of witches or the passage of their goods into the hands of the prosecutors, and Scot conceded that it was better than the "popes lawes." But he notes that in spite of the wisdom of Parliament and the goodness of the queen some English writers plead for Continental severity and that interrogations and trials could go unfairly for witches (13).

Bodin on the law. Scot spends his indignation chiefly, though, on Bodin's formulations for investigation and prosecution, which Scot makes out to be monstrous. "Excommunicat persons, partakers of the falt, infants, wicked servants, and runnawaies are to be admitted to beare witness . . . because (saith Bodin the champion of witchmongers) none that be honest are able to detect" witches (15). Heretics and witches may accuse but not excuse a witch, and "one lewd person . . . may be received to accuse and condemne a thousand suspected witches." Even a "capitall enemie" may testify against the accused, and the rule of law that declares testimony from a single witness insufficient for a death sentence does not hold. Accusers may stay anonymous, presumptions and conjectures can be proof enough, and demonstrated perjury will not invalidate testimony. These and a dozen other outrageously one-sided provisions for trial of witches Scot professes to find in Bodin's *Demonomanie*. Although Scot overstates his case, the truth certainly seems to be that witches could get very bad treatment in Continental courts and, Scot seems to hint, in English ones (16–18).[19]

Confessions and law. The evidence that prosecutors strove for was, of course, confession; they seek it, Scot thinks, by pure entrapment. "If she confess manie things that are false, and one that is true," she dies for the last. An "equivocall or doubtful answer is taken for a confession." A confession later retracted is still held good. And the reason Bodin gives for "this extremitie" is the magnitude of hell's conspiracy: "not one among a thousand witches is detected." And yet, the *Malleus* affirms that "there is not so little a parish but there are manie witches knowne to be therein" (19). Although with other criminals "certeine points of their confessions may be thought erronious, and imputed to error: yet in witches causes all oversights, imperfections, and escapes must be adjudged impious and malicious, and tend to hir confusion and condemnation" (20). And if any "man, woman, or child doo saie, that such a one is a witch; it is a most vehement suspicion (saith Bodin) and sufficient to bring hir to the racke: though in other cases it be directlie against lawe" (20–21).

The sum of Scot's survey is that witches had little hope in the law. "The onlie pitie they shew to a poore woman in this case, is; that though she be accused to have slaine anie bodie with her enchantments; yet if she can bring foorth the partie alive, she shall not be put to death" (21). At this leniency Scot marvels, for he would expect them to say that the devil could deceive the court in the dead man's likeness.

In the succeeding book Scot again goes into the matter of confessions, mostly to show that the deeds confessed to strain all honest credulity. "It is so horrible, unnaturall, unlikelie, and unpossible; that if I should behold such things with mine eies, I should rather thinke myselfe dreaming, dronken, or some waie deprived of my senses; than give credit to so horrible and filthie matter" (46). And anyway, Scot says a few chapters later, the law holds that in capital cases "we must not absolutelie stand to the confession" if it is of an act "impossible both in lawe and nature." Though those who so confess "may be worthy of punishment, as whereby they shew a will to commit such mischeefe, yet not worthie of credit, as that they have such power" (54).

Belief in Witches Idolatrous

Scot is acknowledging here, as he does repeatedly though inconspicuously, that the kind of witch whose existence he affirms can be (however innocent of demonry) an objectionable and harmful person for whom he seeks no immunity from the normal penalties of the law. As he indicates more than once, the witch may be deceitful, venal, malicious in practice upon the credulous, and guilty of arson, poisonings, and treason. At the end of his Epistle to the Readers, Scot says firmly that as for those who in "verie deed are either witches or conjurors, let them hardlie suffer such punishment as to their fault is agreeable, and as by the grave judgement of the law is provided." He speaks, plainly, of those professionals who hire themselves out to lift spells or sometimes to lay them, and to find lost objects, foretell the future, and do other farfetched services. Scot's aim here and later is to draw the clients of witches— and in his view this includes witchmongers—into the company of the accused. He thus used his foes against themselves, for one of their most agreed-upon articles was that whoever resorted to a witch became a witch.

In an early chapter of the *Discovery* Scot says: "I . . . cannot perceive what it is to go a whoring after strange gods, if this be not . . . He that attributeth to a witch, such divine power, as dulie and only apperteineth unto GOD (which all witchmongers doo) is in hart a blasphemer, an idolater, and full of gross impietie, although he neither go nor send to hir for assistance" (9). And in his second Epistle (xvii) he asks, "Is not one manifest kind of Idolatrie, for them that labor and are laden to come unto witches to be refreshed? . . . trulie it is manifold idolatrie, to aske that of a creature, which none can give but the Creator. . . . There should be none of these cousening kind of witches, did not witchmongers mainteine them, followe them, and beleeve in them and their oracles" (xviii).

Bodin convicted. The peak of Scot's success in making his novel case came, perhaps, when late in the *Discovery* he treated an event that Bodin had taken very seriously: the finding of three "images in a donghill to the terror & astonishment of manie thousand." According to Bodin, the English ambassador to France reported there that one of the images was of Queen Elizabeth. Presumably it signified an attempt upon her life.[20] Scot claims that "if such bables could have brought those matters of mischeefs to passe, by the hands of trators, witches, or papists; we should long since have beene deprived of the most excellent jewell and comfort that we enjoy in this world." He admits, though, that ineffectual as the images were, "the feare, conceipt, and doubt of such mischeefous pretenses may breed inconvenience to them that stand in awe of the same. And I wish, that even for such practises, though they never can or do take effect, the practisers be punished with all extremitie" (399).

With this sternness recorded, Scot then turns the whole matter against the witchmongers and other users of witches. The three images in a "donghill" were found to be an attempt not on the queen's life but on the virtue of three women whom a "yoong Gentleman" was pursuing at great expense through the art of an "old cousener." Achieving no results, the gentleman tried at last to recover his money by confessing all to the authorities and so got himself into trouble that Scot held well deserved (400). Bodin in his portentous account of the affair either did not know of the outcome or chose to ignore it. Scot used the episode to expose not only the cozening old witch and his lecherous client but also Bodin, whom he linked with the "yoong Gentleman" in a practice and a gullibility that Scot stoutly calls idolatrous. Thus he turns a charge that Bodin and many others had brought against witches upon the theoreticians who made it and so indicted them equally with the superstitious employers of witches.

Witches not idolaters.   Genuinely deluded witches, Scot had decided, were wrongly called idolaters. "The furtherest point that idolatreie can be stretched unto, is, that they, which are culpable therein, are such as hope for and seeke salvation at the hands of idols, or of anie other than God. . . . But witches neither seeke nor beleeve to have salvation at the hands of divels" (55).

Whether or not Scot thus clears some witches of idolatry, he certainly seems to involve both their users and their special accusers with them in whatever religious offenses witches are guilty of. Those theorists, Catholic and Protestant, who almost to a man cry out against resort to witches for even benevolent services and who believe the services real, are themselves superstitious and so in a sense resorting to witches. Scot's extension of the witch fault to the witchmongers for their God-depreciating credulity and their labors to establish it in all minds was a polemical stroke without precedent in English publication.

Chapter Six

Scot's Reception in England

Tracing the reaction of English writers to Scot's *Discovery* both in his lifetime and in the century following suggests the country was not ready for him when he wrote but that it became increasingly receptive throughout the seventeenth century. Those concerned with the application of laws on witchcraft were bound to have great difficulty with his relaxed recommendations about witches, and both theorists of witchcraft and ordinary Bible readers felt attacked and indignant. Many cultivated and "liberated" persons who shared such lenient views as those of Erasmus and Montaigne must have felt with Gabriel Harvey that Scot unmasked "sundry egregious impostures" and in many passages "hit the nayle on the head." But they might also have agreed with Harvey that Scot did not refute Bodin with either due courtesy or full effectiveness.

Scot and the Law

In implying that England's courts could handle witch cases as they did any other criminal ones, Scot was, perhaps, disingenuous. He depended upon some suppositions about witchcraft that were disagreeable to his time and its laws and that he must have known were rather impracticable. They are, in fact, not even yet established upon the rock of science, however they suit our own time's positivistic view of "spirits." In the late sixteenth century, belief in the occult was more spontaneous than unbelief and seemed, too, more intellectually justified. Uncertainties about witches and spirits were then considerable; some are not even now fully resolved.

To assume before we begin to examine a particular case that no person has psychokinetic powers and that no "separated spirit" has the least ordinary ability to work in the physical world seems to us safe and useful. To Scot it seemed manifestly "true," and he proclaimed it with magnificent resolution. But for an Elizabethan court to throw out all testimony to the evils of witches was to affront general "knowledge" and to leave witch-afflicted persons defenseless short of direct reprisal. A large proportion of England's population was enough convinced of the power of witches for that by itself to bestow a kind of power, and many witches incontestably applied it. Beyond such psychological leverage they may, for all we know, have really possessed now and then some sort of occult force.

How could a court sift testimony that by definition might originate largely from deep error of the senses? The very issue before the court was partly whether in fact such befuddlement had taken place. If a black weasel spoke to a woman in the forest just before she mysteriously took sick what weight should her testimony have to link the two events to a witch? In the early eighteenth century such difficulties were a factor in the courts' withdrawal from the evidence-sifting task with the assumption, unacceptable in the sixteenth, that whatever errors the senses were subject to, none was owing to their basic control by witches acting through devils. But in Scot's day few men felt enough at ease with the malice of a witch to assume with confidence that she could not do him arcane mischief.

Scot and nearly all other defenders of witches stress the malice of their accusers, but a witch's malice carried into court could be as functional against an accuser, if the trial was "fair," as his against her. She could accuse him of bringing the charge out of simple hostility or self-interest. The complainant might, of course, be able to exhibit real injuries, but the job of either tracing them to her or freeing her from connection with them was so hopeless with all legal safeguards in place that it was best simply not undertaken. To Elizabethan juries, though, and apparently to witch-conscious judges and prosecutors the evidence of *maleficia* was as clear-cut, as "generally known," as evidence ordinarily is in difficult criminal cases. The unlikeliness of the connection between the witch and the injury was not troubling, for who knew how far-reaching a witch's demonstrated rancor might be—or a devil's? Perhaps no judge could equitably assume in 1590 that every bewitchment was delusion stemming from ignorance, derangement, or deception unless he was ready to do what the eighteenth-century statute did:

reject every charge under the old witch law before it could be brought, much less tried.

England's statutes on witches caught up with Scot's skepticism in 1736. No one, the new law said, could any longer be prosecuted for "Witchcraft, Sorcery, Inchantment, or Conjuration," though anyone claiming to have or to use power by them could be.[1] Only then could juries legally agree in court with Scot that the witch's marvels were impossible.

Scot's reasons and the new law's were empiricist. As we have seen, no person whom Scot could trust ever surely watched anybody fly on a broomstick, turn into a wolf, become invisible, bring up a storm, or kiss the behind of a real devil. So as a matter of experiential knowledge these things did not happen, and by ready inference they did not because they could not. Experience of men's bodies was that they were too heavy to fly, too fixed in form to turn lupine, too solid to be invisible. The disproportion between a storm and a man was so evident as to discourage conviction that he could control it. But Scot's reasons evaporated for those who could believe despite experience that somewhere people did indeed kiss a real devil's behind and come into his service, as a vast amount of testimony and acute speculation said they did. In the opinion of his foes Scot's experiential check was insufficient simply because the things he denied were rare and secret; the devil's work was hard to grasp or describe, but real. And in fact, Scot could no more establish the demonological negative than believing demonologists could the startling positives that they confidently tossed about.

Scot's Problems with Demonology

Irreconcilably at odds with the dominant thinkers on witchcraft, Scot did not, as we have noticed, bother to writhe his way through the subtleties upon which they depended. His efforts to establish his central thesis that the devil, being a spirit, could not act in the bodily realm touched only rarely and briefly on the much-disputed questions about the nature of spirits and their powers. In the *Discourse* all he could do when at last he expressed his own opinion was, as we have seen, to cite Calvin and Peter Martyr disingenuously and then once more to deride the *Malleus Maleficarum*. For us the derision serves. For his co-evals he was flying impertinently in the face of scripture and of other respected works and of what seemed more than ample recorded "experience" of devils.

Scot's effort to reinterpret biblical episodes with spirits and to discredit secular ones by exposing contradictions or sheer folly in the telling seems at its most self-evidently successful when he points to the habit witchmongers had of picking confirmatory instances from fiction. Transformation of man into wolf "(saith Bodin) is woonderfull: but yet (saith he) it is much more marvellous, that men will not believe it. For manie poets affirme it" (72). How disconnected Bodin is from reality, Scot indicates, to suppose that Homer's tale of a witch turning men into swine meant that witches might indeed perform such a feat (73)!

Bodin's literary examples. But it ought not surprise us that Bodin's usage was not quite the naive one that Scot thought. What Bodin says is that all the people of the earth and all antiquity are agreed on the reality of transformations. Together with poets—Homer, Vergil, and Ovid—he names Herodotus, Strabo, Pliny, and several others. He was, in short, just doing something that his age respected in polemic: bringing up the troops, displaying the thrust of educated opinion and his own credentials in learning.[2]

On how the marvelous in fiction inspires acknowledgment of it in nature, Bodin says briefly that Apuleius in his famous story of a man turned into a donkey enriched his tale with some pleasant devices that were yet no stranger than the realities that Bodin told of.[3] What Bodin seems to have intended at bottom with his reference to *The Golden Ass* and the *Odyssey* was to offer them as examples of skillful and revered narration that opened the mind of the reader to a view of the world that was not routine, every-day, unimaginative. In a similar way modern historians and philosophers sometimes use powerful fiction to reveal convincingly the detailed psychological realities of, say, slavery or the violence of the frontier or the cruelties of concentration camps. *War and Peace* is more "true" to war and peace than most histories can be, though it has unhistorical latitude in dates, names, and geography. Bodin did not take Apuleius's treatment of Thessalian witches to be reportage, nor did he suppose the tribulations of the man-ass to be a case history. He used a talented writer who had come across an account of witchcraft in histories or other arresting testimony and had left a piece of fiction that by astute detail and characterization could help make the events of a bewitchment imaginatively comprehensible.

For such a venture to pay off, the reader must, of course, be already receptive to at least the idea of witchcraft, and perhaps he will draw no firm line between the facts in fiction and those in the real world. He will not, either, be one to apply strictly in his reading P. B. Medawar's warning to a young scientist: "the intensity of the conviction that a hypothesis is true has no bearing on whether it is true or not."[4]

Demonological "truth." To Medawar's pronouncement we might add: Neither does the literary force with which a marvel is recounted have bearing on its truth. Medawar speaks, of course, of the tested and usable (though adjustable) "truth" of scientific hypothesis. Despite the labors of our parapsychologists such truth is hardly conceivable even yet for phenomena once ascribed to witchcraft and devildom. In Scot's time it was hopelessly out of reach, and even the idea of it was scarcely formulated. When in the middle of the seventeenth century Henry More campaigned for "spirit" by trying to give proofs "no less than the mathematical," he relied, unsuccessfully, on a self-extending series of "axioms." Joseph Glanvill, who handled the flank of the contention that depended on the direct evidence of case histories, had no cameras, no recorders, no instruments of any kind to test the memories of witnesses and the deflecting "intensity of the conviction" that they felt—much less any that he felt. And the phenomena that he investigated were ones for which incompetence of the senses was a given.[5]

A century later David Hume proposed a touchstone for miracles: unless the testimony to a miracle was such that for it to be false would be a greater miracle than the one testified to, we may not believe. Hume meant that we may never believe, for the witness to a miracle speaks of an event whose definitive quality is that it is partly beyond our powers to "experience" it. Hume just added an impossible judgment of value to an already insoluble problem of observation. Intensity of conviction will unquestionably have a great deal to do with any observation of marvels and with judgment on them. We may suppose, too, with Bodin, that the skill of the testifying will contribute something to conviction. Also, as the influential nineteenth-century rationalist John Fiske wrote, "The contemporaries of Bodin were so thoroughly predisposed by their general theory of things to believe in the continual intervention of the Devil" that they easily credited any particular event to it, whereas "to the educated man of today such intervention seems too improbable to be admitted on any amount of evidence."[6]

Scot's "general theory." Every thinking man probably develops his own "general theory" out of what is persuasive to him as organized, whether positively or negatively, in the general theories prominent in his time. For him to go far beyond them, particularly in polemic on a popular issue, is very hard. Scot's general theology appears to have been largely that of Calvinism, Bodin's public one in his *Demonomanie* that of orthodox Catholicism.[7] To most of us now Medawar's scientific rationalism will seem more soundly based than the religious faith of Scot and Bodin, for the scientist tests his theories by experiment and use. He quantifies them in a way that little or nothing in religion is susceptible of, as Hume amply pointed out. But when Scot and Bodin believed in divine miracles (with as much conviction as a zoologist does in evolution) Hume's skepticism was not part of any influential general theory. Scot did write off demonic marvels in a way not much different from Fiske's. But to complain, as some modern writers do, that Scot did not have Medawar's reasons for doing it and that he did not, like Hume, abandon God's miracles along with those of witches is to demand far too much of him.

Scot's successes against the *Malleus* and Bodin and the rest were considerable, and the passage of time has augmented them in history. But they were pragmatic. Scot was disputationally superior to his opponents only in common sense. To be sensible, though, was all that he sought and all that, against great odds, he urged on others.

Scot's Self-Thwarting Public Appeal

Scot's common sense about witchcraft did not quench in him what must have been a very strong curiosity about it. As we have seen, he read extensively, and when he wrote he gave far more notice to the works he resisted than anyone did to his work for a long time. For the most part, witchmongers dismissed Scot briefly as a Sadducee, an atheist, or just conceivably another witch. The feature of the *Discovery* that best demonstrates Scot's curiosity and that kept most writers of Scot's own time from grappling closely with the book was its pages of explicit formulas of invocation and of devils' names. Like Bodin, many feared to read such matter. John Cotta, an English physician publishing a modified belief about witches some thirty-odd years after Scot, said that he would write nothing of magical ceremonies, "partly because they are difficult to detect, except by the Witches owne free confession . . . partly, because they tend more to the satisfaction of curiositie than of use, and therefore are not without some danger published."[8]

The suspect material Scot offered, of course, in the derisive spirit that dominated the rest of his treatment of magic's pretensions. But most readers attracted to or impressed by such revelations of ritual seemed to take it as seriously in the *Discovery* as if they read it from the Solomonic *Lemegeton* itself. "Scot's satirical and censorious comments and marginal notes," says E. M. Butler, "were powerless to deglamorize proceedings which have a certain charm even today, and which in his own times were fraught with fascination."[9] Whether as Scot copied incantations or read them over by candlelight he felt any thrill of a magician's interest and waited in uncertainty to see if a devil would appear we cannot know. But the net effect for his readers was not in line with the rationalistic bent of the *Discovery*.

An indication of the effect of the occult material on seventeenth-century readers appears in the addition in 1665 of a highly credulous second book to the *Discourse of Devils and Spirits* and of nine chapters to the beginning of book 15 of the *Discovery*, including blasphemous conjurations. Butler has designated the unknown author of these excrescences "Anti-Scot" because the views that he chaotically expounds are opposed to most that Scot tried to do against witchcraft and magic. Butler supposes that the occult passages in both Scot and Anti-Scot were influential in English literature because they were a poetic improvement on their Hebrew, German, and French originals. However that may be, Anti-Scot's were evidently designed to improve English

sales figures. The 1665 title page has it that they are "conducive
to the completing of the Whole Work," a claim that can only
mean that they are a concession to public interest. The new
book of the *Discourse* begins with a condescending paragraph
explaining that Scot "hath only touched the subject superficially"
and that it "requires most amply to be illustrated" (492). The
writer of the more ample illustration has plainly composed both
fast and recklessly, like a fanatic or a hack seizing an opportunity.[10]

As Butler says, it is "ironical that the only readily accessible
collection in English of ritual process should be enshrined in
the pages" of Scot's skeptical work. It was also unfortunate for
Scot's purposes, since it undoubtedly colored the suspicions of
many that the author's consideration for witches might be that
of a confederate. King James, although he accuses Scot only
of maintaining the "old error of the Sadducees, in denying of
spirits," held Weyer a witch for printing much the same material
that Scot did.[11]

Scot and the Experts

This rather ill-founded discrimination on the king's part may
make us wonder whether he had read the *Discovery* with anything
like the diligence that Scot gave to Bodin, Daneau, the *Malleus*
and the rest. After the accusation in his Preface to the Reader,
the king said no more about Scot and scarcely engaged any of
his specific contentions, though the two authors did, of course,
stand opposed on most of their larger propositions about witchcraft. Claiming to write against Scot's "damnable opinions,"
the king gave little sign of having examined those opinions.
Conceivably he had the *Discovery* in mind when he dealt with
the argument that if "Witches had such power of Witching
folkes to death . . . there had been none left aliue long sence
in the world, but they." Scot had several times commented
that if witches had the power attributed to them, the rest of
mankind would be very bad off. The point, James retorts, "scars-
lie merites an answere." Simply, God keeps the devil on a short
leash. However he may go "about like a roaring Lyon,"[12] he
cannot kill nearly so many as he would like.

Surprisingly the king seems obliquely to back Scot and Weyer

on another question. Scot flatly rejected the orthodox demonological notion that devils are organized in known and elaborate
ranks. James too says that persistence of rank among fallen angels
is simply devilish pretense; it deceives both witches and
demonologists.[13] Such demonic wiliness was, of course, precisely
what Weyer had based his defense of ignorant witches on, and
the untrustworthiness of orthodox demonology is a strong refrain in Scot's argument.

Unless these and a few similar parallels indicate some real
notice of Scot's book, James shows none in his text.

William Perkins. Other prominent witchcraft writers of
Scot's time were equally reticent. George Gifford, who was
mildly of Scot's opinion about some items of doctrine on witches,
never mentions Scot in his *Dialogue,* nor does the influential
Calvinist preacher, William Perkins, in his sermon printed as
A Discourse of the Damned Art of Witchcraft. The Rev. Thomas
Pickering, who published Perkins posthumously, does mention
Scot on the third page of the Epistle Dedicatorie. "That Witches
may and doe worke wonders, is euidently prooued: howbeit
not by an omnipotent power, (as the gainsayer hath unlearnedly
and improperly termed it) but by the assistance of Sathan." A
marginal note identifies Scot as the "gainsayer" and gives a
reference that, being examined, overthrows Pickering's complaint. Scot does indeed twice use the word "omnipotencie"
in his discussion of witches' powers, but he ascribes it not to
witches but to God. It is rather the witchmongers, he indicates,
who extoll "witches omnipotencie" and derogate from "Gods
glorie" (xxv).

Perkins himself, in expounding "false" opinions, habitually
names none of their holders. He gives attention, however, to
several arguments that are in both Scot's work and Weyer's.
"Gainsayers" contend, according to Perkins, that no binding
contract is possible between human beings and "the Deuill"
because "man is bound in conscience to God" and because
the witch is corporeal and Satan spiritual. But all "unlawful
compacts" are contrary to conscience, and a binding one is possible between man and spirit—witness God's with Adam, renewed
with Abraham and his seed. Although the devil does sign a
witch in "fraud and deceit," that does not prove the pact unbind-
ing, but only unlawful. Witches, Perkins concedes, sometimes

"confesse of themselves things false and impossible," such as that they pass through keyholes, are turned into animals, and "are brought into farre countries to meete with . . . the Deuill." But such confessions come from witches who are deep into their contracted time and have by habit become the devil's vassals. They "are deluded, and so intoxicated by him, that they will run into thousands of fantasticall imaginations." Satan can indeed do many "reall workes," Perkins stoutly reminds us, but not nearly so much as a besotted witch may believe.[14] All this and more like it could well be in response to Scot and Weyer, but Perkins never acknowledges them.

Like other English witchmongers, the majority of them clergymen, Perkins mentions few writers of any sort. He prefers to take his authority from the Bible and occasionally from the Fathers. Of others he mentions only Pico della Mirandola, Nicholas Remy (a French judge most credulous about witches after having examined and condemned some 900 of them), Homer (to aver that Circe was just like English witches), and Josephus.

George Gifford. Gifford, a few years earlier than Perkins, cites no authority whatever except scripture. His hundred-page dialogue is about villagers as well as with villagers. Butter-making and the health of stock and parishioners or the stresses of the decaying traditional system of village charity did not grip Perkins. Gifford's primary interests, on the other hand, are first the injustices that local quarrels and suspicions fasten on defenseless old women, and second, the part in those injustices that is played by supposed "good" witches, whom Gifford prefers to call "cunning men." On the first matter Gifford is almost entirely in agreement with Scot. On the second he sounds, as we have seen, like Weyer with his sights lowered. Gifford seems to take seriously the bond of cunning men to the devil. Whether he believed the devil's claw literally busy in cunning men's cures and detections or was just shaping his very cogent dialogue to fit the deep credulity of his rustics is hard to guess. At any rate, Gifford gives no explicit credit to the *Discovery*, though his irony is reminiscent of Scot's. In the *Dialogue*, "the good wyfe R." declares that "some thinke" the witch to be in their cream, so they thrust a red-hot spit into it as they say: "If thou beest there have at thine eye!" Well, replies the skeptical M.D.: "If she were in your creame, your butter was not very cleanly."

A dog, mistaken for a devil and charged in the name of the Trinity "to tell what he was . . . at last told them, for he sayd . . . bowgh, and thereby they did know what he was."[15]

Gifford shares one anecdote with Scot. Both tell, though without any verbal similarities, of a woman who "had bleare eyes" cleared up by a charm hung about her neck. She was forbidden to read it, but eventually "another" did read it: "The divell pluck out thine eyes, and fill their holes with his dung." Scot and Gifford rejoice in this example of cozenage, but both grant that sometimes such charms do work if the beneficiary believes in them.[16]

Like Scot, Gifford felt that the old women accused of *maleficia* were more sinned against than sinning. But Gifford seems to have held that the devil did actively delude them, whereas Scot put the blame for erroneous confessions on "melancholie" and on abuse from their neighbors and the law. Gifford does not refrain from condemning such abuse, particularly from uncharitable neighbors, who with only faulty evidence suspect and accuse and who sit as jurors to convict. Gifford does not, like Scot, blame the law for allowing prejudiced witnesses, but he does condemn hearsay evidence and all testimony from the devil, who, he indicates, is virtually the author of the misguided suspicions and confessions that abound in witch trials.[17] In Germany, the wise Daniel of the *Dialogue* explains, devils cause witches to suppose that "they raise tempests . . . kill both men and beasts . . . are turned into wolves . . . meet together and banquet, that sometimes they flie or ride in ayre, which things indeede are nothing so."[18] Gifford evidently knew about Continental witchcraft, but unlike Scot he does not pay it much attention.

How, asks the interlocutor, is a jury ever to convict a witch if all her vile deeds are just devil-inspired fantasy? She ought to die, Daniel responds, not for killing by poison that the devil supplies, but simply for dealing with devils. If a jury finds proof of that it should convict her. But, objects M. B., for that offense the law will not allow hanging them, and Daniel acknowledges that the law should be improved so as to "cut off all such abominations." Then we find, however, that the devil-dealing that Daniel abominates is not that of malefic witches but that of the "cunning man" who, "seeming to do good" to those be-

witched, draws "the people into manfold impieties."[19] Here
Gifford certainly parts from Scot's view that the cunning man
is just a mercenary fraud.

Gifford ends his "slender treatise" with a passionate and rather
irritable fifteen-page plea for jurymen to convict upon hard evidence only, not upon surmise and likelihood.[20] With this Scot
no doubt agreed, though Gifford's argument is pitched much
lower than his. Gifford wrestles with farmers, Scot largely with
learned Continentals. Gifford never used Scot's word "impossible" in connection with witches' feats, though he does say that
a jury is not to credit a witness whose "oth cannot be true."
Immediately, though, he himself credits the word of a man
who thought that a huge devil's face hovered over him in his
bedroom one night. It, says the pious and learned Daniel, was
"indeed" an "illusion of the divell."[21] Gifford concludes on
an almost embittered note when "the good wife R.," rejecting
Daniel's mild wisdom, accused the almost liberated M. B. of
defending witches and hopes that his "nagge might hault a little"
so that she could see whether he "would not be glad to seeke
help" from cunning persons. She closes the argument with a
final intransigent question: "doth not Gods word say there bee
witches, and doe you not thinke God doth suffer bad people?"

The one vital item of witch doctrine that Gifford accepted
and Scot rejected is the physical meddling of devils in men's
ordinary affairs. Gifford never touches on the means of it, so
we may assume if we like that at heart, anyway, he was of
Scot's party. But he does not say so.

Others of Scot's time. The difference between Gifford
and Scot appears in the undistinguished *Treatise against Witchcraft*
(1590) of Henry Holland, who speaks well of Gifford but thinks
that Scot cut witchcraft down unjustifiably to just a "cozening
or poisoning art." He is right, of course, but shows no recognition of the virtues of the reduction. Like others he allows Scot
only a single dismissing mention.[22]

The English witchcraft writers, then, who published between
the first edition of the *Discovery* and the death of Scot gave
him no open attention beyond some passing words of rebuke.
A few other writers mention him. Thomas Nashe in *Four Letters
Confuted* (1592) shrugs off the charge against his own *Pierce*

Penniless Supplication to the Divel that it is a "diabolicall Discourse" with the remark that in a "far fetcht sense" the *Discovery* might be similarly accused, though it is certainly antidiabolical.[23] In the next year Gabriel Harvey conceded that the *Discovery* "dismasketh sundry egregious impostures." But he could have wished that Scot "had dealt somewhat more courteously with Monsieur Bodine, or confuted him somewhat more effectually."[24] Considering the size and force of Scot's work, the recognition it received was very slight.

Opinion to mid-century. Not long after Scot's death, two clerical demonologists backing Samuel Harsnett in his controversy with the Puritan exorcist John Darrell named Scot among their "seueral Authors" and used him occasionally. Like him they emphasized that the Witch of Endor was a ventriloquist who deceived Saul, and they cited approvingly Scot's ridicule of *Lemegeton's* catalog of devils. Darrell in his answer notes that they used "Skot" and so probably did not believe in witchcraft.[25]

Harsnett himself, then chaplain to the Bishop of London, was for a long time Scot's most imposing admirer among English writers. He used the *Discovery* favorably in a marginal note of his 1603 *Declaration of Egregious Popish Impostures.* One historian calls him a disciple of Scot, and another says that Scot "colored his thought."[26]

Famous Continental witchmongers—Nicholas Remy, Henri Boguet, Martin Del Rio, Pierre de Lancre—made no mention of Scot. Nor did Pierre Le Loyer (the first book of whose *Discours des Spectres* was translated into English in 1605) in his more than one hundred pages of discussion on the existence and apparition of spirits.

In 1616 the comparatively liberal John Cotta says of Scot in a marginal note that "erroneously he confoundeth . . . as one and the selfe-same sinne" imposture and witchcraft, and again that *"Reginald Scott* doth overabound" in examples of "lying pretense" in magic.[27] Eleven years after Cotta, Richard Bernard in the Dedication to his *Guide to Grand-Jurymen . . . in Cases of Witchcraft* protested a rumor that he "were of Master Scots erroneous opinion that Witches were silly Melancholikes." In 1646 John Gaule felt much the same about Scot, though he seemed to hold many opinions very like Scot's.[28]

Opinion after 1650

After the middle of the century, however, the witchmongers lost much ground in England. Though they continued to dominate publication, some of them seem to have been moved more than before to take some detailed notice of their opponents, though they were still disdainful. Thus lordly though not very attentive was Meric Casaubon in his long argumentative introduction to John Dee's account of passages with "some spirits." He admitted that he himself had not read Scot but attacked him just the same. "I have heard some men magnifie" his book written "to prove that there be no Witches." Casaubon relies on the derogatory opinion of the learned Dr. John Reynolds. Some thirteen years later, still without having read Scot, Casaubon classes him among "confident illiterate wretches."[29]

Filmer and Ady. Not all the notice that Scot got in Casaubon's time was adverse. He had about as many and as able defenders as detractors, and he steadily gained in recognition and influence as the century passed. Obviously sympathetic to Scot's views, though he is not explicit about any debt, was Sir Robert Filmer, who in 1653 published *An Advertisement to the Jurymen of England* on the difficulties of knowing what a witch was and who was one. Three years later Thomas Ady's *Candle in the Dark* also had warnings for jurymen. Ady resisted all witchmongering, especially that of Perkins, and followed Scot so openly that a historian calls him "even more than Filmer . . . a disciple of Scot."[30] Plainly Ady was that. He repeatedly appealed to Scot and defended him—neither of which Filmer did. Like most of the worthier of his kind Ady seems moved primarily by compassion and common sense. But neither compelled him, any more than they had Scot, to cast off Bible-authorized belief in spirits and to deny real meaning to the word *witch,* once he had stripped it of traditional nonsense. Ady made much of Scot's acknowledgment of the existence of witches of a sort, however it might exclude most of their peculiar feats. The "opinion that witches are not" Ady says roundly, was "neither [Scot's] tenent nor is it mine."[31] Apparently one thing both Ady and Scot had in mind was to sound a bit more orthodox on witches than they were.

Scot's late defenders. After the ambiguous republication of the *Discovery* and the *Discourse* with occult supplements in 1665 the literary controversy over witchcraft entered its final years. Casaubon, Henry More, Joseph Glanvill, Richard Baxter, and some others launched a rally for spirits against a growing resistance by John Wagstaffe, an anonymous author rather uncertainly identified as a New Englander named N. Orchard, and John Webster, who was the most imposing and effective of them. They stood together and with Scot through hot exchanges in the 1670s and 1680s.

Orchard scathingly, if in somewhat veiled fashion, assailed all witchmongering. In the course of a rather obscure sneer at Casaubon's attack on Scot, Orchard calls Scot "the Chief and First *Anti-demonologist* of this *Nation* at least."[32] Like Scot, Orchard held witchmongering to be "idolatrous." Wagstaffe wrote of the plight of accused innocents and of the absence from scripture of real evidence on witches. His book was reprinted once in England with additions and later translated into German.[33]

John Webster, the most noticed of the antidemonologists, was well acquainted with the work of Scot and Weyer and of Ady, Wagstaffe, and Orchard. He also knew and resisted as much of Casaubon, More, and Glanvill as had appeared by 1676. To Casaubon's churlish slurs upon Scot, Webster answers that "the falsity of this foul scandal is manifest . . . for Mr Scot was a learned and diligent person . . . he understood the Latine tongue and something of the Greek, and for the Hebrew . . . had very good helps." Webster noted that the little treatise "titled *Daemonologia,* fathered upon King James" (Ady had named the Bishop of Winchester as the real author)[34] "intimated" Weyer and Scot "to be Witches"—an accusation that should elicit only "scorn and derision, as having no rational ground of probability." But, sighed Webster, Glanville, carrying on the slander, said that Scot, witchlike, "denied the existence of Witches," whereas the fact known to anyone who read him was that he denied only the powers ascribed to witches. Glanvill, "who pretends to such high parts," had used the false charge, Webster thought, to convict Scot of Sadduceeism or atheism.[35]

Webster noticed that Glanvill also "throws upon" Scot that he "doth little but tell odd tales and silly Legends, which he confutes and laughs at. . . . In all which, his reasonings are trifling and childish; and when he ventures at Philosophy, he is little better than absurd." Well, shrugs Webster, if the tales are indeed silly, notice that Scot took them from such as Del Rio, Bodin, and the *Malleus*, "the Authors that are most esteemed with Dr. Casaubon, and other Witchmongers." Should Scot be "little better than absurd, then he the better agrees with Mr Glanvill, whose Platonicall Whimseys are as absurd as any."[36]

In his preface Webster grandly claims that Weyer, Scot, Ady, Wagstaffe, and others had "pretty well quashed and silenced" witchmongering in England until Casaubon and Glanvill "raked up the old arguments." Webster attacked Henry More, too, saying that he depended on "stories that seem . . . fabulous, impossible, and incredible." Of these stories Webster ironically names "that of the Pied-Piper" as More's most believable.[37]

More and Glanvill.   More and Glanvill were not the men to let these or any other published disagreement with them go unanswered. Glanvill counterattacked at some length, and More did at great length in late editions of the best-selling *Sadducismus Triumphatus*. They pounced especially upon Scot's account of the Witch of Endor, which Webster had praised. Glanvill had attacked it already in the first edition of the *Sadducismus*, so that Webster in a chapter on "the Woman of Endor that pretended to raise up Samuel" undertook to "confute his arguments."[38] More came to Glanvill's help in a long letter full of high disdain for the scholarship of Scot and his followers and a show of his own great learning. He labeled Webster's book "weak and impertinent" and in thirty-five pages full of Latin, Hebrew, and complaints about Webster's rendering of both, he chopped the Endor story up fine. Scot's reduction of the "Pythoness" to a trickster working with a confederate "knave" More finds "against all sense and reason . . . against the inspired Scripture itself"; and he called Scot, Ady, and Webster "sworn Advocates of the Witches." The question was then whether in the ordinary course of life after death Samuel could have appeared in person and how. This was More's special ground, and he argued that the dead have "both a Faculty and a Right to move of themselves." They have "a power of appearing in their own personal shapes" and also a "Care or Regard for those they left on earth." He established his opinion deviously out of *Tobit*, in which the angel Raphael rescued Tobias from a killer devil. Webster may ask, More admits, "What is all this to the Purpose, when the Book of *Tobit* is Apocryphal, and consequently of no Authority?" More answers witheringly: "Certainly of infinitely more Authority than Mr. *Wagstaffe*, Mr. *Scot*, and Mr. *Adie*, that Mr. *Webster* so frequently and reverently quoteth."[39]

Glanvill's responses to Scot and Webster were less pretentious than More's. In his "Proofs of . . . Witches from Holy Scripture" in the later editions of the *Sadducismus* Glanvill discussed Scot's "evasion . . . concerning the Witch's Closet" with the comment that Scot, the "father of modern Witch-Advocates," is not "interpreting a Story, but making one; for we read nothing [in scripture] of her *closet* . . . or of Saul's standing at the Door like a . . . drowned Puppy, as Mr Webster has it."[40] Glanvill then more temperately, more briefly, and perhaps more effectively than his ally did, argued against Scot's opinion.

The dying controversy. The most evident fact about the whole controversy in the late seventeenth century is that the parties to it, for all their learning and intensity, made no headway. The subject as defined simply had no room for much new. Scot's case on the Witch of Endor and on witchcraft in general was perhaps a little bumptious, but it was full, self-consistent, lucid, and largely new. The followers he won could not extend it appreciably without utterly dismissing devils from existence and with them great ranges of what was understood of spiritual evil itself. Scot had already reduced these things as far as traditional regard for biblical authority could allow. Although he had broadcast the ideas of demonographers to show how fantastic they were and how they induced terrible persecutions, the central religious facts of one God and of supreme evil were no fantasy to Scot. Nor were they to Webster and the rest. Deistic tendencies were waxing in England, but not among the antidemonologists, who had trouble enough without readjusting the concept of deity and revelation. Nor did their opponents want such adjustment. Henry More was a latitudinarian about the church. But in his views of spirits the latitude was simply the freedom to restate "scientifically" and most elaborately the nature of matter and spirit to the advantage of the latter. Perhaps too, like Scot, More applied psychological explanation a bit more freely to biblical story than most of his predecessors did.

The controversy laid to rest. In the Dedication of the 1720 edition of his *Historical Essay Concerning Witchcraft* the Rev. Francis Hutchinson sums it up: "That tho' the sober Belief of good and bad Spirits is an essential Part of every good Christian's Faith, yet imaginary Communications with them, have been the Spring both of the worst Corruptions of Religion, and the greatest Perversions of Justice."[41] He thus states the sufficient ground for the repeal that followed in a decade and a half of England's law on the prosecution of witches. His remark could stand, too, as a summary of the position that Scot so clear-headedly took. Belief in angels, good and evil, was a Christian given; belief in witches was a commonsense acknowledgment of an observed fact in society that the law recognized. But, as Scot and Hutchinson knew, a fearful misapprehension about "communications" between devils and witches perverted both criminal law and religious piety; and it curdled mercy in the hearts of thousands. Scot was helpless to make a controlled study after the fashion of modern social scientists, but he could and did achieve clear and practical concepts based on personal investigation of cases available to him and on shrewd interpretation of stories in the literature. Just how influential he was in stopping the witch craze we can never know; but as it abated, the public mood certainly came more and more into phase with Scot's lucid empiricism on both physical and psychological matters.

A Dutch clergyman, Balthazar Bekker, usually gets credit for the witchcraft controversy's burial service. Like Scot, he cleared devils out of worldly action without depriving the Christian of faith in them. Bekker's stand was more difficult than Scot's, however, and at least as doubtful, and not a bit better founded theologically. Instead of denying finite spirits' physical powers he simply declared that after Eden God had confined Satan and his host to hell. This was demonology that, like Scot's, sweepingly disposed of demonology, and apparently Bekker's world was about ready to accept it—or at least to accept its consequences.[42]

An English writer who fruitlessly resisted Bekker in 1705 was John Beaumont. In capsuling Bekker's arguments, Beaumont translates the Dutchman as acknowleding very handsomely that he finds no earlier author who "has ascribed so little understanding and Vertur to the Devil, as for what relates to all those Knowledges and Effects set forth by me, as *Reginald Scot.*" Bekker aligns himself with Scot and "many others, who are opposite to the Belief Men have of [the devil's] power."[43]

So the demonological struggle faded away with Scot come into his own but soon to be forgotten except by historians.

In Retrospect

One hundred forty years after Beaumont's anachronistic effort against Bekker, English historians were beginning to speculate on the documents of witchcraft. The editor of a county-society reprint of some witch pamphlets thought it "curious and edifying to observe to whom mainly we owe enlightened views" on witchcraft. We might have expected them from "the recognized guides of public opinion . . . the Bacons, the Raleighs, the Seldens, the Cudworths, and the Boyles." But these distinguished thinkers seemed to acquiesce in conventional witch doctrine, so that we owe our debt to a "strangely assorted and rather grotesque band" that provided a "vindication of outraged common sense and insulted humanity." On the four men of this band (Scot, Filmer, Wagstaffe, and Webster) "a literary Pharisee would look down with supercilious scorn." A "country gentleman . . . deep in platforms of hop gardens" led them. He "gives no quarter to the delusions . . . throws . . . discredit and ridicule upon the whole system," shows "an extraordinary elevation of good sense." Scot was not, the editor concedes, a scholar "in the sense in which the term is applied to the Scaligers, Casaubons, and Vossius's. . . . But he had original gifts far transcending scholarship . . . a manly, straightforward, vigorous understanding . . . an honest integrity of purpose . . . admirable mother-wit and single-minded sincerity." The editor admits, though, that Scot "only scotched the snake instead of killing it."[44]

Since the time of that editor dozens of comments have echoed his opinion of Scot or parts of it. Scot, they say, was not a superior scholar, but he was sensible, vigorous, honest, and he did do the snake some damage. Why then did he not kill it? Because he did not take his skepticism far enough, or because he took it too far for his time. Perhaps because he "panders" to the public's interest in the occult, or is too hard on Catholics. Or, Montague Summers seemed to think, simply because he was egregiously "wrong" in his whole case and would have been more wrong still if he had dared.

Summers on Scot. Summers gives the opinion of some authority whom he does not name (but who is apparently Summers himself) that the "fatal flaw" in Scot's argument is denial of demonic activity in the world—a "sufficiently illogical position." The real fact, Summers says, is "that although for caution's sake covering his atheism with the thinnest veneer . . . [Scot] wholly and essentially denies the supernatural." Scot's "citations," too, are "second-hand" and irrelevant, and he is "very dull, narrow, and ineffective."[45] Summers obviously opposed Scot in much the same way that Henry More did; what Scot had to say was so objectionable to him that he was blind to its merits.

As much of Summers's indictment of Scot as is objectively verifiable—the assertion that Scot's references are "second-hand and irrelevant"—does not stand up, for the references are mostly to be found in the originals as Scot gives them, and they seem appropriate. As witchcraft writers go, too, Scot is certainly not dull. Narrow? Well, his was not a spacious intellect. He was not eager to explore inscrutable possibilities; unearthliness troubled him; he did not delight in the supernormal. But then, the supernormal that Scot rebelled against was unattractive to most of the intellects of his time that *were* spacious. Its study was without real advance since the time of Aquinas and gave convincing signs of being fictitious in many of its claims and cruel in some results.

Was the *Discovery* "ineffective"? If, as one modern historian says, it was "brilliant," or, as another one has it, far ahead of its time, and Scot himself, according to a third, "the greatest of the witch-hunters' enemies"[46] why did the mania continue largely unchecked for a century after his publication?

The large answer is, of course, obvious. No writer fighting to make a case strange to his public and contrary to its received opinion is likely to effect a quick and sweeping change—especially if his book is burned within twenty years of publication and remains substantially out of print for another fifty years. During his lifetime and for long after, Scot does not seem to have had much standing with most other writers on his subject. But after 1650 he certainly got much notice, most of it favorable. To judge from the later editions of his book he must, too, have had a large general readership. He was clearly effective in the years in which belief in witchcraft was wearing away to nothing.

Opinion on Scot's stand on spirits. Of Summers's slurs on Scot the only one much in question now is whether Scot really does "wholly and essentially" deny the supernatural, though for caution's sake covering his "atheism," and whether his stand, whatever it may have been, was to his credit. Lynn Thorndike in his monumental work on magic and science seems to hold Scot's skepticism flawed by an unbecoming acknowledgment of "fascination" (a kind of built-in witch's power like the "evil eye") and by an effort to "satisfy . . . interest in occult arts and magic." Keith Thomas mentions, apparently with approval, "Scot's view that Satan was merely a symbol of man's evil temptations." Sydney Anglo, the most authoritative recent writer to concentrate upon Scot, decides that he does reduce finite spirits to metaphor and therefore was in fact a Sadducee in his view of spirits. Anglo notices Scot's occasional explicit declarations of faith in spirits. But he seems to think that the more numerous and extended passages in which "Scot himself has interpreted them metaphorically" overpower the conventional concession that they are individual beings.[47]

Certainly Scot took pains to establish that the word *spirit* may have various meanings in scripture, including the metaphorical. "For sometimes . . . spirits and divels are taken for infirmities of the bodie; sometimes for the vices of the mind; sometimes also for the gifts of either of them. . . . sometimes for the teachers and prophets; sometimes for zeale towards God; sometimes for joie in the Holie-ghost, &c" (427). But here, too, Scot enters his disclaimer: "I denie not therefore that there are spirits and divels, of such substance as it hath pleased GOD to create them. But in what place soever it be found or read in scriptures, a spirit or divell is to be understood spiritualie, and is neither a corporall nor a visible thing" (428).

Must these invisible and incorporeal created spirits, then, be only metaphorical? Scot repeatedly asserts otherwise. Sadducees are "impious and fond" to hold that "spirits & divels are but notions, and that angels are but tokens of God's power." Scot confesses, with Augustine, that these matters are above his reach. Still, as we have seen, so "farre as Gods word teaches" him, he will "not sticke to saie, that they are living creatures, ordeined to serve the Lord in their vocation. Although they abode not in their first estate, yet that they are the Lords ministers, and executioners of his wrath, to trie and tempt in this world, and to punish the reprobate in hell fier in the world to come" (453).

Does Scot make this statement just for "caution's sake, covering his atheism," his "total rejection of the supernatural"? Anglo speaks disdainfully of Summers's opinion, but he himself seems to indicate that Scot was at least evasive about his doctrine of spirits. Anglo says, too, that Scot fell into "circularity of argument" when he denied all demonic marvels and at the same time affirmed the miracles of God as "historically true." How could he "know that they were true"? To answer that the Bible is divine revelation "simply begs the question."[48]

Scot on miracles. So as Summers holds that Scot covers up apostasy, Anglo holds that he disappointingly flinches from it. Anglo apparently would prefer that Scot show boldly the atheists' colors that Summers thought he kept cravenly furled. The fact is, though, that Scot, like most Christian writers of his time, saw no contradiction in accepting miracles while rejecting magic. For by a commonplace of theology, miracles and magic were conceptually distinct—miracle the work of the almighty Creator, magic that of creatures, whether witches or devils or the two in alliance. Most writers on magic, including those who believed in it as well as in miracle, make the distinction. Thus John Cotta: "It is the propertie of the Diuel, in his seeming miraculous contriuements . . . (though a limited and finite . . . creature of God) yet to indeuor to counterfeit . . . workes of wonder of the infinite Creator . . . the true miracles of God being transcendent aboue all created power." And William Perkins explains that transmutation is "a work simply above the power of nature, and therefore cannot be done by the deuill or any creature. For it is the proper work of God alone . . . to create, to change, or to abolish nature." The devil could do only certain "lying wonders" from his special knowledge of nature.[49]

Except that he cuts the devil off completely from temporal action, Scot himself said repeatedly about miracles and magic the same thing that Cotta and Perkins did. Scot cited, for instance, a celebrated canon of the medieval church that they who believe that "anie creature can be . . . transformed . . . by anie other than by God himselfe the creator of all things . . . is an infidel" (77). He called attention to the fact that Christ, not necromancers, raised the dead.

Why, then, is it a contradiction for Scot to reject the superstition of demonic marvels while holding to divine miracles—unless we are to think that he ought empirically to have confounded the two? But that, surely, is not a clarification reasonable to expect of Scot or of any sincere Christian.

To find, then, either a cover-up or a flinching in Scot's opinion on devils as not instrumental in magic is to go against the logic of all orthodox theology of Scot's time. Disbelief in the devil's corporeal power and belief in God's creative power are not inconsistent. If, of course, we ask how Scot "could know" that biblical miracles "were true," the sufficient answer is that he knew by faith, not by circling his logic. If God created Lot's wife, as Scot "knew" he did, then surely he could turn her into salt.

Scot on the existence of witches. Trevor-Roper is another modern historian who praises Scot but finds that his "doctrine" left the "witchcraze . . . logically . . . untouched." Scot thus failed because he did not attack the craze "at its centre . . . challenge the whole conception of the kingdom of Satan." Scot never declared that "witches do not exist, not even that the pact with Satan is impossible."[50]

The fact is, though, that Scot did declare pact impossible, and he did deny the existence of witches in any form that might justify the witchmongers. Furthermore, he made these declarations not once and ambiguously, but repeatedly and plainly. Consider his Epistle to the Reader: "Naie, bicause I bewraie the follie and impietie of them, which attribute unto witches the power of God: these witchmongers will report, that I denie there are anie witches at all: and yet behold, (saie they) how often is this word Witch mentioned in the scriptures. Even as

if an idolater should saie in the behalfe of images and idols,
to them which denie their power and godhead . . . How dare
you denie the power of images, seeing their names are so often
repeated in the scriptures? But truelie I denie not that there
are witches or images: but I detest the idolatrous opinions conceived of them . . ." (xxv–xxvi). How could anyone make himself clearer or more positive? Scot did deny that any such witches
exist, as Trevor-Roper thinks he should deny. And he continued
to deny it throughout his book.

    Scot on pact. Book 3 Scot gave mostly to the pact, largely
to the absurd details of it as much-prompted confessions had
laid them out. But chapter 4 he headed: "That there can be
no reall league made with the divell. . . ." He then forthrightly
denied this "bargaine, that (they say) is made betwixt the divell
and the witch," though "manie of great learning conceive it
to be a matter of truth, and in their writings publish it according-
lie: the which (by Gods grace) shall be proved as vaine and
false as the rest" (31). And later in the book: "But whie should
there be more credit given to witches, when they saie they
have made a reall bargaine with the divell . . . than when she
confesseth that she transubstantiateth hir selfe? . . . But you
see the one to be impossible, and therefore you think thereby,
that their confessions are vaine and false" (45–46). And so
through book 3 and the whole of the *Discovery* and the *Discourse*
Scot firmly and consistently made his case.

A Tribute

    One of the most just brief appreciations of Scot's work by a
British historian came from W. E. H. Lecky over one hundred
years ago:

. . . he unmasked the imposture and the delusion of the system with
a boldness that no previous writer had approached, and with an ability
which few subsequent writers have equalled. Keenly, eloquently, and
unflinchingly, he exposed the atrocious torments by which confessions
were extorted, the laxity and injustice of the manner in which evidence
was collected, the egregious absurdities that filled the writings of the
Inquisitors, the juggling tricks that were ascribed to the Devil, and
the childish folly of the magical charms. . . . If the question was to
be determined by argument, if it depended simply or mainly upon

the ability or the learning of the controversailists, the treatise of Scott would have had a powerful effect; for it was by far the ablest attack on the prevailing superstition that had ever appeared, and it was written in a popular style.[51]

Lecky's treatment of Scot is so brief that he gives himself no chance to make errors of detailed interpretation. But his tribute was surely well deserved.

Notes and References

Chapter One

1. The justice's reference to a learned person from the Continent is much commented on by historians. See Wallace Notestein, *A History of Witchcraft in England from 1558 to 1718* (Washington, D.C., 1911), p. 46. The justice's warning to the witch is recorded in a notorious pamphlet, *A true and just Recorde of the Information, Examination, and Confession of all the Witches taken at St. Oses* [Osyth]. . . . By W.W. 1582. It is included entire with modernized spelling in *Witchcraft*, ed. Barbara Rosen (London: Edward Arnold, Ltd., 1969), pp. 121–22.

2. H. R. Trevor-Roper, *The European Witch-craze of the Sixteenth and Seventeenth Centuries* (New York, 1967), p. 138; Notestein, *History*, pp. 14–15.

3. Ibid., p. 16.

4. Ibid., p. 18, says that Jewel was the man that the justice referred to years later, but Rosen's conjecture, p. 121n, that it was the celebrated French witch writer Jean Bodin seems much more likely.

5. Montague Summers, *The Geography of Witchcraft* (New York, 1927), p. 495.

6. The Protestant Thomas Erastus, whose demonology, at least, was orthodox in the Thomistic manner, says that since only God and finite spirits can act above nature and God and good angels do not serve magicians, devils must be their agents. *Deux Dialogues de Thomas Erastus, Docteur en medicine a Heidelburg, touchant le pouvoir des Sorcieres*, printed with Iean Wier [Weyer], *Histoires disputes et discours, des illusions et impostures des diables, des magiciens infames, sorcieres* (Paris, 1579), p. 808.

7. Neither the Sabbat nor the notion of "any sect or cohesive group" of witches appears in Aquinas. See Charles Edward Hopkin, *The Share of Thomas Aquinas in the Growth of the Witchcraft Illusion* (Philadelphia: University of Pennsylvania Press, 1940), p. 176.

8. See E. M. Butler, *The Myth of the Magus* (Cambridge, 1948), p. 162.

9. See A. L. Rowse, *Sex and Society in Shakespeare's Age* (New York: Scribners, 1974), pp. 35–36, on Simon Forman's practice in magic and his troubles with the law.

10. See Keith Thomas, *Religion and the Decline of Magic* (New York, 1971), p. 443.

11. For Weyer see the Paris, 1885, reprint of the 1579 *Histoires,* pp. 135–36. For Bodin the Paris, 1598, edition of the *Demonomanie,* pp. 2–4.

12. Proclus, *De Sacrificia et magia,* printed with *De Mysteriis Aegyptiorum, Chaldaeorum, Assyriorum,* tr. from the Greek by Marsilio Ficino (Lyons, 1577), p. 280.

13. C. L'Estrange Ewen, *Witchcraft and Demonianism* (London, 1933), pp. 157–58, 162.

14. See Daneau's Introduction, sig. B4.

15. Joseph Leon Blau, *The Christian Interpretation of the Cabala in the Renaissance* (New York, 1944), p. 44.

16. Thomas, *Religion,* pp. 234–37.

17. Ewen, *Witchcraft,* pp. 142–43.

18. Paracelsus (Theophrastus Bombastus von Hohenheim), *The Archidoxes of Magic,* trans. Robert Turner (London, 1656), p. 81.

19. See Christopher Baxter, "Johann Weyer's *De Praestigiis Daemonum:* Unsystematic Psychopathology," in *The Damned Art: Essays in the Literature of Witchcraft,* ed. Sydney Anglo (London: Routledge & Kegan Paul, 1977), p. 59.

20. Ibid., p. 57.

21. See ibid., pp. 58–59, for Weyer's rejection of high magic, both Hermetic and Cabalistic.

22. Erasmus, *The Praise of Folly,* trans. Hoyt Hopewell Hudson (Princeton, N.J.: Princeton University Press, 1941), pp. 54–57, 73–79. See also Trevor-Roper, *European Witch-craze,* p. 130, and Frances A. Yates, *The Occult Philosophy in the Elizabethan Age* (London, 1979), p. 53.

23. "Of Cripples," *The Complete Essays of Montaigne,* trans. Donald M. Frame (Stanford, Calif.: Stanford University Press, 1965), pp. 784–92.

24. See D. P. Walker, *Spiritual and Demonic Magic from Ficino to Campanella* (London, 1958), pp. 107–11, and Sydney Anglo, "Reginald Scot's *Discoverie of Witchcraft:* Scepticism and Sadduceeism," in *The Damned Art,* pp. 132–34.

25. All references here to the *Discovery* and to *The Discourse of Devils and Spirits,* which was bound with the *Discovery* and paginated continuously with it, will be from the only complete modern edition, that magnificently edited by Brinsley Nicholson and published in London in 1886.

26. *The Malleus Maleficarum of Heinrich Kramer and James Sprenger,* translated with Introductions, Bibliography, and Notes by Rev. Mon-

tague Summers (New York, 1971), p. viii. Summers declares the *Malleus* to be "among the most important, wisest, and weightiest books of the world." All further references to it will be to this translation. The *Canon Episcopi* seems to have been issued not in the fourth century but about the year 900.

27. Scot's late contemporary, Samuel Harsnet, who ended life as Archbishop of York, was among Englishmen who knew Bodin and admired his work before he wrote against witches. See Harsnet's *A Declaration of Egregious Popish Impostures* (London, 1605), p. 132.

28. References are to the Bodley Head reprint of 1924, a line-for-line and page-for-page reproduction of the original, edited by G. B. Harrison.

29. *A Discourse of the Subtill Practises of Deuilles by Witches and Sorcerors* (London, 1587); *A Dialogue Concerning Witches and Witchcraftes* (London, 1593). References to Gifford's *Dialogue* are from the 1603 edition as reprinted by the Percy Society, 1842.

Chapter Two

1. See the introduction to the Nicholson edition of the *Discovery*, p. xxv. The information below on Scot's life is from Nicholson, except as otherwise specified, including his convenient reprinting from Wood's *Athenae Oxonienses*. Very little is available on Scot's life.

2. Ady was one of Scot's defenders. The quotation is from p. 87 of the second edition of the *Candle*, which was retitled *A Perfect Discovery of Witches* (1661).

3. See A. L. Rowse, *The England of Elizabeth: The Structure of Society* (New York, 1951), p. 102.

4. Quotation is from the first edition of *A Perfite Platform of a Hoppe Garden and necessarie Instructions for the making and maytenance thereof . . . made by Reynolds Scot* (London, 1574), p. 8. Subsequent references will be in the text.

5. Rowse, *England*, p. 219.

6. Ibid., p. 101.

7. Ibid., p. 38.

8. Ibid., p. 230.

9. Ibid., p. 341.

10. Ibid., pp. 344–47.

11. See Joseph H. Marshburn, *Murder and Witchcraft*, (Norman: University of Oklahoma Press, 1971), for contemporary accounts of criminal activities and prosecutions between 1550 and 1640.

12. Rowse, *England*, p. 355.

13. Ibid., pp. 342–43.

14. See Dr. John Dee, *The Private Diary*, ed. James Orchard

Halliwell (London, 1842), and William Perkins, *Discourse of the Damned Art of Witchcraft*, in *The Works* (London, 1613).

15. See Dee's *Diary*, p. 10. For Harsnett see note 27 of chapter 1 above.

16. See, for instance, Wayne Shumaker, *The Occult Sciences in the Renaissance* (Berkeley, 1972), chapter 1, especially pp. 9–12.

17. In a marginal note Scot seems to say that he took his catalog of demon princes from a manuscript done by "one T.R." in 1570 (p. 327). According to Anglo, Weyer's *Pseudomonarchia* was first published in 1577; according to Butler (*Ritual Magic*, p. 65), in 1563. Either way, of course, Scot could have used it, and he does refer to it just before he begins his catalog of demons.

18. See Nicholson, *Discovery*, p. xxxv.

19. *Malleus*, p. 118.

20. *Demonomanie*, p. 192.

21. Ibid., p. 216.

22. *Malleus*, p. 188.

23. See chapter 6 on increasing support for Scot in the seventeenth century.

24. See Thomas, *Religion*, p. 572.

Chapter Three

1. Norman Cohn, *Europe's Inner Demons* (New York, 1977), Preface. Cohn expands his views throughout the rest of the book. He stresses the distorting effect of tortures—as does nearly every other modern writer on witchcraft. For an excellent brief treatment see Trevor-Roper, *European Witch-craze*, pp. 117–23.

2. Cohn, *Europe's*, pp. 169–75. For the view that Scholastics did hold magic and witchcraft to be at bottom one, see Jeffrey B. Russell, *A History of Witchcraft* (London, 1980), pp. 12–14.

3. Cohn, *Europe's*, p. 193.

4. Ibid., pp. 170–71.

5. On Faustus as at once magician and witch see Robert H. West, "The Impatient Magic of Dr. Faustus," *English Literary Renaissance*, Spring 1974, pp. 218–40. As Edward Peters says in *The Magician, the Witch, and the Law* (Philadelphia, 1978), p. 165, "Although both anthropologists and historians persist in separating the crimes of magic and witchcraft, medieval theologians and lawyers did not."

6. See Charles Edwin Hopkin, *The Share of Thomas Aquinas in the Growth of the Witchcraft Delusion* (Philadelphia: University of Pennsylvania Press, 1940).

7. Cohn, *Europe's*, p. 115.

8. Thomas, *Religion*, pp. 521–22.

9. Cohn, *Europe's,* pp. 58–59.
10. Ibid., pp. 228–29.
11. Trevor-Roper, *European,* pp. 122–25.
12. The witchcraft indictments, depositions, and confessions recorded in C. L'Estrange Ewen's *Witch Hunting and Witch Trials* (London, 1929), and *Witchcraft and Demonianism* provide ample evidence that English horror of witchcraft was not wholly a matter of *maleficia.*
13. Alan Macfarlane, *Witchcraft in Tudor and Stuart England* (New York, 1970), p. 189.
14. Thomas, *Religion,* pp. 441–49.
15. Macfarlane, *Witchcraft,* pp. 147–89.
16. Thomas, *Religion,* p. 555.
17. Ibid., p. 552–53.
18. Alan Macfarlane, "A Tudor Anthropologist: George Gifford's *Discourse and Dialogue,*" in *The Damned Art,* p. 151.
19. Keith Thomas, "Anthropology and the Study of English Witchcraft," in *Witchcraft Confessions and Accusations* edited by Mary Douglas, (London: Tavistock Publications, 1970), p. 58.
20. Thomas, *Religion,* p. 497.
21. Ibid., p. 498.
22. Ibid., pp. 563, 565.
23. Ibid., p. 557, 552.
24. Jeffrey Burton Russell, *Witchcraft in the Middle Ages* (Ithaca, N.Y., 1972), pp. 233–34, and Rossell Hope Robbins, *The Encyclopedia of Witchcraft and Demonology* (New York, 1959), pp. 9, 144.
25. Richard Baxter, "Jean Bodin's *De la Demonomanie des Sorciers,*" in *The Damned Art,* p. 78, and Thomas, "Anthropology," p. 58, and *Religion,* p. 564. See also G. L. Kittredge, *Witchcraft in Old and New England* (Cambridge, 1929), p. 25.
26. Thomas, *Religion,* pp. 564–67.
27. Macfarlane, *Witchcraft,* p. 3.
28. Cohn, *Europe's,* pp. 261–62.
29. Ibid., pp. 228–29.

Chapter Four

1. *Summa Contra Gentiles,* Bk. III, Pt. ii, ch. 106, p. 75, as excerpted in *Witchcraft in Europe, 1100–1700,* ed. Alan C. Kors and Edward Peters (Philadelphia: University of Pennsylvania Press, 1972), p. 61. Aquinas relies here for his information about magicians on Porphyry's *Letter to Anebo.*
2. This argument, the last clause verbatim with Scot, appears in Ludvig Lavater's *Of Ghostes and Spirites Walking by Nyght,* trans. R. H. (London, 1572), ed. J. Dover Wilson and May Yardley (reprint

ed., Oxford: Oxford University Press, 1929, p. 134). Lavater explained that the argument troubled Augustine but need not have, since Ecclesiasticus was not a canonical book.

3. The Geneva headnote for I Samuel 28 says that the Witch "causeth Saul to speak with Samuel." See also Andrew Willett, *An Harmonie upon the First Booke of Samuel* (Cambridge, 1607), p. 313.

4. Scot gives no marginal reference for the *Malleus*, which speaks twice of David's harping away Saul's devil, both times attributing success simply to the fact that the harp "was made in the sign of a cross." See Pt. I, Q. 5, p. 41, and Pt. II, Q. 2, ch. v, pp. 178–79.

5. See Joseph B. Collins, *Christian Mysticism in the Elizabethan Age* (Baltimore: The Johns Hopkins Press, 1940), especially pp. 170 ff. For Vane see *The Retired Man's Meditations, or the Mystery and Power of Godliness* (London, 1655), and for John Pordage, *Theologia Mystica* (London, 1683)—published long after Pordage's death.

6. Hugh Ross Williamson, ed., *Discoverie* (Carbondale, Ill., 1964), p. 19.

Chapter Five

1. See Blau, *Christian Interpretation*, chapter 6, "The Fantastic Cabala," especially p. 87.

2. Some of this chapter Scot lifted verbatim or nearly so from the English translation of Agrippa's *De Vanitate*, called *Of the Vanitie of Artes and Sciences*, trans. J. Sanford (London, 1569; reprint ed., Northridge, Calif.: 1974), ed. Catherine M. Dunn, pp. 131, 134, 380–81. The angel Riziel seems to be Scot's ironic invention.

3. See the *Vanitie*, p. 128.

4. On Ficino see Walker, *Spiritual and Demonic Magic*, pp. 40 ff.; and Yates, *Occult Philosophy*, p. 45. For Reuchlin and Pico, see ibid., pp. 23–24.

5. On Pico's *Apologia* see Blau, *Christian Interpretation*, pp. 24–25, and Yates, *Occult Philosophy*, p. 20. For magic as within nature see Ernst Cassirer, *The Individual and the Cosmos in Renaissance Philosophy* (New York: Harper & Row, 1963), pp. 110, 149–50.

6. Yates, *Occult Philosophy*, p. 47; Walker, *Spiritual and Demonic Magic*, p. 75.

7. Henry Cornelius Agrippa, *Three Books of Occult Philosophy*, trans. J.F. (London, 1651), p. 358.

8. *The Fourth Book of Occult Philosophy or Magical Ceremonies*, trans. Robert Turner (London, 1655), pp. 88, 84.

9. *Heptameron or Magical Elements*, trans. Robert Turner (London, 1655), pp. 117–18.

10. Bodin, *Demonomanie*, p. 117.

11. Ibid., p. 118.
12. Anglo, "Scot's *Discoverie*," p. 119.
13. Gilbert, *De Magnete* (London, 1600), pp. 68, 208, 211, as cited by Walker, *Spiritual and Demonic Magic*, p. 79.
14. Boyle, "An Hydrostatical Discourse," in *The Works* (London, 1744), pp. 276, 288.
15. Aquinas notices the distinction in Damascene. *Summa Theologica*, Q. 50. Art. I. Peter Martyr, *The Common Places* (London, 1574), pp. 113, 80–88.
16. *A Commentary upon the Prophecie of Isaiah*, trans. C.C. (London, 1609), p. 6.
17. Calvin in his *Commentary* on Isaiah, p. 14, had noticed this misinterpretation as a "most absurde blockishnesse" of Papists.
18. Scot never acknowledges it, but Bodin had said the same of Satan. *Demonomanie*, pp. 4 ff.
19. For Bodin on evidence and trial procedures see *Demonomanie*, Book IV, chapter ii.
20. See Ibid., p. 254. Kittredge, *Witchcraft*, pp. 87–78, says that the Spanish ambassador to England gave his government details of this "Islington scandal" and that Ben Jonson mentioned it in *The Masque of Queens*.

Chapter Six

1. Hole, *Witchcraft*, p. 147.
2. Bodin, *Demonomanie*, p. 215.
3. Ibid., p. 219.
4. P. B. Medawar, *Advice to a Young Scientist* (London: Harper & Row, 1980), p. 47.
5. Henry More, *The Immortality of the Soul* (London, 1659), and Preface to *Collection of Several Philosophical Writings* (London, 1662), p. xv. Joseph Glanvill, *Sadducismus Triumphatus*, 4th ed. (London, 1726), pp. 270–446.
6. John Fiske, *Outline of Cosmic Philosophy Based on the Doctrine of Evolution* (Boston: J. R. Osgood & Co., 1875), p. 379.
7. In private Bodin seems to have departed idiosyncratically from Christianity toward a kind of Judaism. See Walker, *Spiritual and Demonic Magic*, pp. 171 ff; Baxter, "Jean Bodin's *Demonomanie*, pp. 83 ff; Marion Leathers Daniels Kunz, Introduction to Bodin's *Colloquium of the Seven about Secrets of the Sublime*, trans. Kunz (Princeton, 1975), pp. xxiv ff.
8. John Cotta, *The Triall of Witchcraft* (London, 1616), p. 79.
9. Butler, *Ritual Magic*, p. 235.
10. See the analysis of Anti-Scot's work in Robert H. West,

Milton and the Angels (Athens: University of Georgia Press, 1955), pp. 61 ff.

11. King James, *Daemonologie in Forme of a Dialogue* (Edinburgh, 1597), Preface, pp. xi, xii.

12. Ibid., p. 30.

13. Ibid., p. 21.

14. William Perkins, *Discourse of the Damned Art of Witchcraft* (London, 1613), p. 612.

15. George Gifford, *A Dialogue of Witches and Witchcraft* (London, 1593), pp. 117, 98.

16. Ibid., pp. 68–69; Scot, *Discoverie,* pp. 198–99.

17. Gifford, *Dialogue,* pp. 92, 96 ff.

18. Ibid., p. 94.

19. Ibid., p. 95.

20. Ibid., pp. 99 ff.

21. Ibid., p. 107.

22. Notestein, *History,* p. 72n.

23. Thomas Nashe, *Strange News of the Intercepting of Certaine Letters* (London, 1592), in *The Works,* ed. Ronald B. McKerrow (reprint ed., New York: Oxford University Press, 1958), ed. F. P. Wilson, 1:308–9. The 1593 edition was retitled *Apologie of Pierce Penniless.*

24. Gabriel Harvey, *Pierce's Supererogation* (London, 1593), ed. A. B. Grosart, *The Works,* (London, 1884; reprint ed., New York: AMS Press, 1966), 2:291.

25. John Deacon and John Walker, *Dialogicall Discourses of Spirits and Divels* (London, 1601), "To the godly affected Reader" (no pagination), and pp. 104, 126. John Darrell, *A Survey of Certaine Dialogical Discourses* (London?, 1602), p. 28.

26. Samuel Harsnett, *Declaration* (London, 1605), p. 135. See Thomas, *Religion,* p. 489, and Notestein, *History,* p. 90.

27. Cotta, *Triall,* pp. 62, 66.

28. Richard Bernard, *Guide to Grand-Jurymen . . . in Cases of Witchcraft* (London, 1627), Dedication. John Gaule, *Select Cases of Conscience Touching Witches and Witchcraft* (London, 1646). To Gaule's credit is a very effective resistance to Matthew Hopkins, the witch-hunter.

29. John Dee, *A True and Faithful Relation of What Passed for Many Years between Dr John Dee . . . and Some Spirits* (London, 1659), Preface, A2. Meric Casaubon, *Of Credulity and Incredulity* (London, 1672), pp. 40–41.

30. See Notestein, *History,* p. 241.

31. The second edition renamed *A Perfect Discovery of Witches* (London, 1661), A3. In his "Reason of the Book" Ady speaks at

length and with praise of Scot and throughout cites him admiringly.

32. N. Orchard, *The Doctrine of Devils Proved to be the Grand Apostasy of these Later Times* (London, 1676), p. 195.

33. John Wagstaffe, *The Question of Witchcraft Debated* (London, 1669).

34. Ady, *Perfect Discovery,* p. 140.

35. John Webster, *The Displaying of Supposed Witchcraft* (London, 1677), pp. 12, 9, 10, 37.

36. Ibid., p. 11. Scot never used Del Rio, who did not publish his huge *Disquisitionem Magicarum* until the year of Scot's death.

37. Ibid., pp. 292–93.

38. Ibid., pp. 166–67.

39. Glanvill, *Sadducismus,* pp. 2, 12, 28–31.

40. Ibid., p. 251.

41. Francis Hutchinson, *An Historical Essay Concerning Witchcraft* (London, 1720), Dedication, p. A3.

42. Balthazar Bekker, *De Betoverde Weereld* (*The World Bewitched*) (Amsterdam, 1690). See Trevor-Roper, *European,* pp. 173–75, for a brief discussion of Bekker's work. He thinks that Bekker has received more credit for ending the witch-craze than he should have. Kittredge praised Bekker highly and much prefered his dismissal of devils to Scot's, which he misunderstood. See *Witchcraft,* pp. 341–42, 353.

43. John Beaumont, *Treatise of Spirits, Apparitions, Witchcrafts, and other Magical Practices* (London, 1705), pp. 359–60. He speaks with amusement of Bekker's central principle that "there were Devills once in the World, who corrupted Humane Nature, but since that time, God Almighty put them in chains, so that they have never made any Figure in the World since" (p. 348).

44. *Pott's Discovery of Witches in the County of Lancaster,* ed. James Crossley for the Chetham Society (London, 1845), pp. xi, xii, xiv, xix, xvii.

45. Montague Summers, Introduction to *The Discoverie of Witchcraft* (London, 1930), pp. xxx–xxxii. Anglo, "Scot's *Discoverie,*" p. 138, note 34, says that the authority Summers cites is himself in *The Geography of Witchcraft* (London, 1927), pp. 128–29.

46. See Thomas, *Religion,* p. 54; Notestein, *History,* p. 72; R. Trevor Davies, *Four Centuries of Witch-Beliefs* (New York, 1972), p. 22.

47. Thorndike, *A History of Magic and Experimental Science* (New York, 1929–41), 6:530; Thomas, *Religion,* p. 475; Anglo, "Scott's *Discoverie,*" pp. 134, 138.

48. Anglo, "Scott's *Discoverie,*" p. 133.

49. Cotta, *Triall,* p. 43; Perkins, *Discourse,* p. 612. See also Aqui-

nas, *Summa Theologica,* Of the Assaults of the Demons, Quest CXIV, Art. iv.

50. Trevor-Roper, *European,* pp. 172, 148–49.

51. W. E. H. Lecky, *History of the Rise and Influence of Rationalism in Europe* (New York: D. Appleton & Co., 1870), 1:122–23.

Selected Bibliography

PRIMARY SOURCES

The Discoverie of Witchcraft . . . Hereunto is added a treatise upon the nature and substance of spirits and diuels. London, 1584. The Da Capo Press issued a facsimile of this edition, New York, 1971. Second edition: London, 1651, and 1654, the latter with a slightly variant title page. Third edition: London, 1665, with a second book added to the *Discourse . . . of Devils and Spirits* and nine chapters to the beginning of the fifteenth book of *The Discoverie.* Thomas Basson, an English stationer living in Holland, published a Dutch translation of the *Discoverie* in 1609 and his son G. Basson, a second edition of it in 1637.

The Discoverie of Witchcraft . . . Being a Reprint of the First Edition. . . . Edited with Explanatory Notes, Glossary, and Introduction by Brinsley Nicholson, M.D., Deputy Inspector General. London, 1886.

The Discoverie of Witchcraft . . . with an Introduction by the Rev. Montague Summers. London: John Rodker, 1930. A second printing (paperback) "unabridged and unaltered." New York: Dover Publications, 1972.

The Discoverie of Witchcraft. . . . Introduced by Hugh Ross Williamson. Carbondale: Southern Illinois University Press, 1964.

A Perfite Platform of a Hoppe Garden. London, 1574. The Da Capo Press issued a facsimile of this edition, New York, 1972. A second edition "Newly corrected and augmented": London, 1576. A third edition: London, 1578.

SECONDARY SOURCES

Ady, Thomas. *A Perfect Discovery of Witches.* London, 1661. The first edition was titled *Candle in the Dark:* London, 1656.

Agrippa, Henry Cornelius. *Occult Philosophy.* Translated by J.F. London, 1651. *De Occulta Philosophia* was first published

Cologne(?), 1533, after long circulation in manuscript.

———. *Of the Vanitie of Artes and Sciences.* Translated by Ja. Sanford. London, 1569, reprinted Northridge: California State University Foundation, 1974. Edited by Catherine M. Dunn. *De Vanitate* was first published in 1526.

Beaumont, John. *Treatise of Spirits, Apparitions, Witchcrafts, and other Magical Practices.* London, 1705. This book is among the last by an English witchmonger.

Bekker, Balthazar. *De Betoverde Weereld.* Amsterdam, 1690. Book I was translated as *The World Bewitched:* London, 1695.

Blau, Joseph Leon. *The Christian Interpretation of the Cabala in the Renaissance,* New York: Columbia University Press, 1944. A brief and sound introduction to its subject.

Bodin, Jean. *De la Demonomanie des Sorciers.* 4th ed. Lyon, 1598. The first edition was published in 1580. *Colloquium of the Seven about Secrets of the Sublime (Colloquium Heptaplomeres de Rerum Sublimium Arvanis Abditis).* Translated with Introduction, Annotations, and Critical Readings by Marion Leathers Daniels Kuntz. Princeton, N.J.: Princeton University Press, 1975. The Latin original was not printed until 1875.

Butler, E. M. *The Myth of the Magus.* Cambridge: Cambridge University Press, 1948.

———. *Ritual Magic.* Cambridge: Cambridge University Press, 1949. Butler's books are largely expansions and corrections of the work of A. E. Waite.

Casaubon, Meric. *Of Credulity and Incredulity.* London, 1672. A work of extremely orthodox scholarship on faith in marvels.

Cohn, Norman. *Europe's Inner Demons.* New York: New American Library, 1977 (paper). First edition: New York: Basic Books, 1975.

Crossley, James. Introduction to *Pott's Discovery of Witches.* Reprinted from the original edition of 1613, for the Chetham Society, Manchester, 1845. Kittredge compliments Crossley for making the pamphlet available.

Cotta, John. *The Triall of Witch-Craft.* London, 1616, published in fascimile by Da Capo Press (New York, 1968). Pleads the need for medical consultation in witch cases.

The Damned Art: Essays in the Literature of Witchcraft. Edited by Sydney Anglo. London: Routledge & Kegan Paul, 1977. Excellent essays on ten major works on witchcraft from *Malleus Maleficarum* to Cotton Mather's *Wonders of the Invisible World.*

Daneau, Lambert. *A Dialogue of Witches.* London, 1575. Daneau was the first Continental witchmonger to be translated into English.

Davies, R. Trevor. *Four Centuries of Witch Beliefs.* New York: Benjamin Blom, 1972. Davies blames the Puritans for Jacobean persecution of witches.

Deacon, John, and Walker, John, *Dialogical Discourses of Spirits and Divels.* London, 1601. A long and learned attack on the notion of contemporary possession and exorcism.

Dee, John. *The Private Diary.* Edited by James Orchard Halliwell. London: Camden Society, 1842. Much stray comment on occult matters. *A True and Faithful Relation of What Passed for Many Years Between Dr. John Dee . . . and Some Spirits.* Introduction by Meric Casaubon. London, 1659. A famous example of the seriousness with which able men could seek communication with spirits.

Ewen, C. L'Estrange. *Witch Hunting and Witch Trials.* New York: Dial Press, 1929.

————. *Witchcraft and Demonianism.* London: Heath Cranton, 1933. Ewen was a pioneer in the documentation of witchcraft from court records.

Gifford, George. *A Dialogue of Witches and Witchcraft.* London, 1593. Reprinted from the 2d ed., 1603, for the Percy Society, London, 1842. A facsimile of the first edition was published by the Shakespeare Association, Oxford, 1931.

Glanvill, Joseph. *Sadducismus Triumphatus.* 4th ed. London, 1726. Glanvill began his work on witchcraft in 1666 with *Some Philosophical Considerations Touching Witches.* It grew into the *Sadducismus,* first published under that title in 1681 and expanded with the work of More and others.

Harsnett, Samuel. *A Declaration of Egregious Popish Impostures.* London, 1605. This work was against Catholic exorcists, as Harsnett's earlier one was against the Puritan exorcist John Darrell.

Heptameron or Magical Elements. Falsely attributed to Peter of Abano. Translated by Robert Turner. London, 1655. Bound with the *Heptameron* are other Turner translations, including *The Fourth Book of Occult Philosophy or Magical Ceremonies,* falsely attributed to Agrippa. The Latin originals may be found appended to Agrippa's *Three Books* (Paris, 1567).

Hole, Christina. *Witchcraft in England.* New York: Charles Scribner's Sons, 1947. A short and readable history.

Hopkin, Charles Edward. *The Share of Thomas Aquinas in the Growth of the Witchcraft Delusion.* Philadelphia: University of Pennsylvania Press, 1940. Cohn refers to this dissertation as sustaining his own theories that the Middle Ages knew nothing of the witch as described in the *Malleus.* He was unaware of the publication of Hopkin's work.

Hutchinson, Francis. *An Historical Essay Concerning Witchcraft.* London, 1720. An enlarged edition taken from the 1718 one. The book is sometimes said to herald the end of witchcraft in England.

James I. *Daemonologie in Forme of a Dialogue.* Edinburgh, 1597. Two more editions were published in London in 1603 when James succeeded Elizabeth. An exact reprint was published in London (1924), edited by G. B. Harrison, as Bodley Head Quarto IX.

Kramer, Heinrich, and Sprenger, James. *Malleus Maleficarum.* 1486(?) Translated with Introductions, Bibliography, and Notes by Rev. Montague Summers. London: John Rodker, 1928; reprinted 1948; republished (paper) New York: Dover Publications, 1971. There were twenty-nine editions of the *Malleus* before 1669. In many, other Catholic treatises were incorporated with that of Kramer and Sprenger.

Kittredge, George Lyman. *Witchcraft in Old and New England,* Cambridge, Mass.: Harvard University Press, 1929. This book has almost as many pages of notes as of text and is a mine of detailed information.

Lavater, Ludvig. *Of Ghostes and Spirites Walking by Nyght.* Translated by R.H. London, 1572; reprinted Oxford: Oxford University Press, 1929. Edited by J. Dover Wilson and May Yardley, for the Shakespeare Association. Contains an informative appendix by Yardley on Elizabethan spiritism.

Macfarlane, Alan. *Witchcraft in Tudor and Stuart England.* New York: Harper & Row, 1970. Largely concerned with Essex.

More, Henry. "Letter to Mr Glanville . . . representing to him the marvellous Weakness and Gullery of Mr Webster's Display of Witchcraft." In *Sadducismus Triumphatus,* 1726 ed., pp. 1–35. The greater part of the letter is marked as Postscript and is an exhibit of More's astonishing prolixity.

Notestein, Wallace. *A History of Witchcraft in England from 1558 to 1718.* Washington, D.C.: The American Historical Association, 1911. Still invaluable for obscure names and dates.

Orchard, N. *The Doctrine of Devils Proved to be the Grand Apostacy of these Later Times.* London, 1676. Identification of the author is doubtful.

Perkins, William. *Discourse of the Damned Art of Witchcraft.* London, 1613. Perhaps the witchmongering work that had most weight for Englishmen.

Peter Martyr of Vermigli. *The Common Places.* London, 1574. Peter's works were highly thought of by English Protestants.

Peters, Edward. *The Magician, the Witch, and the Law.* Philadelphia:

University of Pennsylvania Press, 1978. Very good on the relation of magic to witchcraft.

Proclus. *De Sacrificia et Magia.* Printed with *De Mysteriis Aegyptiorum, Chaldaeorum, Assyriorum,* as translated from the Greek by Marsilio Ficino. Lyons, 1577. Proclus and Ficino were much referred to in Renaissance debates on magic.

Rawcliffe, D. H. *Illusions and Delusions of the Supernatural and the Occult.* New York: Dover Publications, 1950. "Scientific" explanations of the marvelous.

Robbins, Rossell Hope. *The Encyclopedia of Witchcraft and Demonology.* New York: Crown Publishers, 1959. Lives up to its title.

Rowse, A. L. *The England of Elizabeth: The Structure of Society.* New York: Macmillan Co., 1951. Authoritative on innumerable details of Scot's Kent.

Russell, Jeffrey Burton. *Witchcraft in the Middle Ages.* Ithaca, N.Y.: Cornell University Press, 1972. Cohn criticizes Russell for his use of some traditional sources but concedes that his scholarship is impressive. See also his brief *History of Witchcraft.* London: Thames & Hudson, 1980.

Shumaker, Wayne. *The Occult Sciences in the Renaissance.* Berkeley: University of California Press, 1972. A valuable survey.

Summers, Montague. *The Geography of Witchcraft.* New York: Alfred A. Knopf, 1927. One of the many books and editions by a learned but astonishingly credulous author.

Thomas, Keith. *Religion and the Decline of Magic.* New York: Charles Scribner's Sons, 1971. Its chapters on witchcraft and magic may be the finest historical work on them in English.

Thorndike, Lynn. *A History of Magic and Experimental Science.* 8 vols. New York: Columbia University Press, 1941. An immense subject treated with commensurate learning. Some errors of detail.

Trevor-Roper, H. R. *The European Witch-craze of the Sixteenth and Seventeenth Centuries.* New York: Harper & Row, 1969. A much-cited long essay first published in 1967 and somewhat revised in 1972.

Walker, D. P. *Spiritual and Demonic Magic from Ficino to Campanella.* London: Warburg Institute, 1958. A lucid account of the theories of magic of Renaissance humanists.

Webster, John. *The Displaying of Supposed Witchcraft.* London, 1677. The strongest of Scot's seventeenth-century supporters, Webster was, strangely enough, also a supporter of the occultist Robert Fludd.

Weyer, Johann [Wier, Iean]. *De Praestigiis Daemonum.* Basle, 1563. An anonymous translation, *Histoire Disputes et Discours, des Illusions* *et Impostures des Diables, des Magiciens Infames, Sorcieres et Empoisonneurs,* Paris, 1579, has an added sixth book. Reprinted with different pagination in Paris, 1885.

Witchcraft. Edited by Barbara Rosen. London: Edward Arnold, 1969. A judicious selection of Elizabethan and Jacobean pamphlets on witchcraft.

Yates, Frances A. *The Occult Philosophy in the Elizabethan Age.* London: Routledge & Kegan Paul, 1979. Occultism from Raymond Lull to John Milton.

Index